Jazz It Up

Judy Murrah

Jazz It Up

101 Stitching & Embellishing Techniques

Edited by Marjon Schaefer

That Patchwork Place®

Jazz It Up

101 Stitching & Embellishing Techniques
Judy Murrah

Copyright© 1998 by Landauer Corporation

This book was designed and produced by Landauer Books
A division of Landauer Corporation
12251 Maffitt Road, Cumming, Iowa 50061

President: Jeramy Lanigan Landauer
Vice President: Becky Johnston
Editor-in-Chief: Marjon Schaefer
Art Director: Tracy DeVenney
Graphic Designer: Laurel Albright
Illustrator: Ann Mackey Weiss
Associate Editors: Marlene Hemberger Heuertz, Sarah Reid
Photographers: Craig Anderson Photography

Published by Martingale & Company
PO Box 118, Bothell, WA 98041-0118 USA

This book is printed on acid-free paper.
Printed in Hong Kong

Library of Congress Cataloging-in-Publication Data
Murrah, Judy, 1943-
    Jazz It Up 101 Stitching & Embellishing Techniques/ Judy Murrah
        p.   cm.
    Includes index.
    ISBN 1-56477-245-4 (softcover)
    1. Patchwork—Patterns 2. Strip quilting—Patterns I. Title.
  TT835.M85 1998
746.46'041--dc21   98-29410
            CIP

10 9 8 7 6 5 4 3 2 1

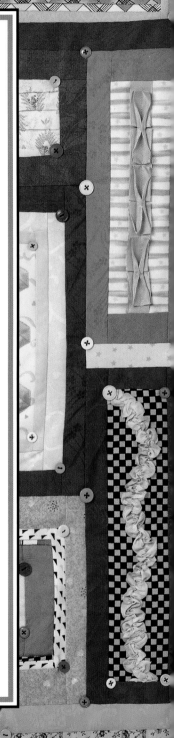

Dedication

To my two older sisters,
Suzanne and Joanie, who
tolerated my constant paste,
paper, and fabric messes
when I was a little girl.

Acknowledgments

My deep appreciation goes to:
My husband, Tom, and daughter,
Holly, for their interest and input
in my work and for helping to
make miracles happen.

David Peha and Nancy Mahoney with
Clothworks for giving me the
opportunity to design a line of fabric.

Marjon Schaefer, my editor,
for her happy attitude.

CONTENTS

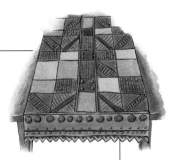

Part 4 • Fabric Embellishing

Part 5 • Manipulating Techniques

Part 6 • Dimensional Techniques

FOREWORD

I love creating bits and pieces of patchwork and then finding a place to use them. As evidenced by the people taking my classes and using my books around the world, you do too. There's so much gratification in seeing the magic happen as you sew together strips of fabric, cut them apart, and rearrange them into another design to be placed among the patchwork.

In my teaching travels, I've talked with my students about how they use my books. The time has come to take the use of the Jacket Jazz books one step further. In *Jazz It Up* you'll find many of the techniques from my other books categorized and put into one book. Look for old favorites and find new ones to make your next fabric collage project. The ideas and steps are here—you be the designer.

Use this book as a workbook; you may want to take it to your local printer and have it inexpensively spiral bound. I've done this to many of my books, enabling me to work from a flat, open book. Make your own notes and ideas in it as you work.

Jazz it Up is not just for garment designers. It's a patchwork of fabric techniques that can be used in making a variety of quilts, pillows, and decorative items as well. Make the patches and build a quilt or garment as you add patches row by row or section by section. You'll see the magic happen right before your eyes.

Judy Murrah

STRIP-PIECING TECHNIQUES
— PATCHWORK BLOCKS —

*Use patchwork blocks as our grandmothers did to make a quilt,
or break down the units into dividing rows for other patchwork
or as a surface embellishment.*

Quilt & Pillow Techniques:

String-Pieced Square Block

Make a row of these blocks to create a secondary pattern as you place blocks next to each other.

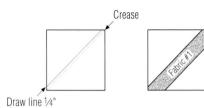

Figure 1

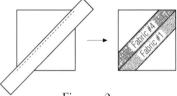

Figure 2

Figure 3

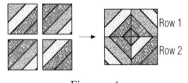

Figure 4

SUPPLIES

1½" x 12" strips each of Fabrics #1, #2, #3, and #4
6" square of muslin or other lightweight fabric

DIRECTIONS

1. Fold the muslin square in half on the diagonal. Press, then open out and draw a line ¼" above the crease. Place a Fabric #1 strip right side up across the muslin square with one raw edge along the drawn line; pin in place. Cut away those parts of the strip that extend beyond the edges of the square. See Figure 1.

2. Place a Fabric #4 strip face down on top of the Fabric #1 strip, aligning one raw edge with the upper edge of the Fabric #1 strip; pin. Stitch through all layers ¼" from the raw edges. This seam should run from corner to corner of the muslin square beneath. Flip the Fabric #4 strip right side up onto the foundation; press carefully, pin in place, and trim. See Figure 2.

3. Referring to Figure 3 for placement, continue adding strips in the same manner until you have used each of the fabrics two times to cover the muslin square. Turn the square to the muslin side and stitch ⅛" from the raw edges. Press.

4. Cut the square into four 3" squares. Place the squares on a flat surface and rotate so the seam lines of the strips form a square in the center. Using a ¼" seam allowance, sew the squares together in two rows, then sew the rows together, forming a 5½" square. Trim the edges if necessary. Press. See Figure 4.

Square Dance

You get two patchwork techniques in one when you use this method.

SUPPLIES

Color Family 1: One 3" x 42" strip each of medium dark, medium light, and light fabric

Color Family 2: One 3" x 42" strip each of medium dark, medium light, and medium fabric

Quilter's Rule Jr.

DIRECTIONS

Note: Cut all strips across the width of the fabric from selvage to selvage. The strips can be pieced if necessary.

1. From each of the fabrics listed above, cut two 1½" wide strips. You will have a total of 12 strips. Sew the strips together in the order shown in Figure 1 to make two identical strip-pieced units of six strips each.

2. Cut six squares from each strip-pieced unit, using the Quilter's Rule Jr. or another 4½"-wide ruler with a 45° line. Place the 45° line along the center seam and cut along the two edges of the ruler. Turn and reposition the ruler so you can cut the third and fourth sides. Save the leftover triangles. Some will be A triangles (Color Family 1) and some will be B triangles (Color Family 2). See Figure 2.

3. Make two rows of five to six squares each, arranging them to form a zigzag pattern. See Figure 3. The number needed depends on the desired length. Sew the squares together into rows and press the seam allowances in one direction. The rows can be sewn together to make one long row to be used as a border, or sew two rows together facing each other.

4. Using a ⅛"-wide seam allowance, sew three sets of two B triangles together with one A triangle between each set. See Figure 4. Make an identical strip. Sew the strips together along the long straight edges. Use as an appliqué patchwork piece.

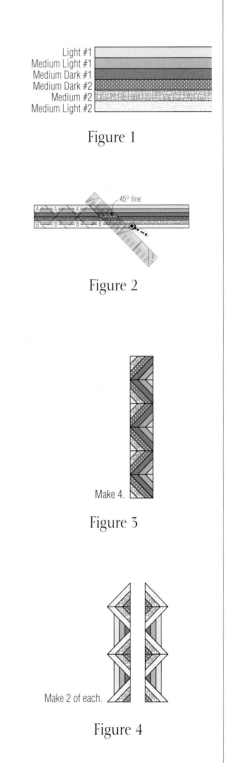

Light #1
Medium Light #1
Medium Dark #1
Medium Dark #2
Medium #2
Medium Light #2

Figure 1

45° line

Figure 2

Make 4.

Figure 3

Make 2 of each.

Figure 4

Magic Maze

This truly is magic when you begin moving around the cut triangles to make your patchwork blocks.

SUPPLIES
⅛ yard each of seven high-contrast fabrics

DIRECTIONS
1. Cut a strip from each of the seven fabrics, varying the widths and cutting each one across the width of the fabric. When sewn together, the resulting strip should be 8" wide.

2. Sew the strips together, using ¼" seam allowances. Strips 1 and 7 will be the most prominent in this piece, so plan accordingly. Press all the seam allowances in one direction.

3. Cut the strip-pieced unit into five 8" squares. If the strip-pieced unit is a little narrower or wider (up to 8½"), cut squares that are a little larger or smaller than 8". See Figure 1.

4. Cut each square twice diagonally to yield four triangles (A, B, C, D). See Figure 2.

5. Lay out two rows of five squares (ten triangles). See Figure 3.

6. Now assemble the triangles into blocks and stitch the blocks together so that you have two sets of five blocks each.

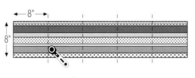

Figure 1

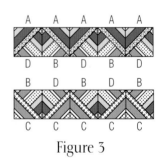

Figure 3

Figure 2

Crossroads

When buying fabric for your quilt add in some extra to make these Crossroads Blocks for interesting borders.

SUPPLIES
3"-wide strips each of
    six fabrics
45° x 90° right-angle triangle

DIRECTIONS

Note: Cut all strips across the width of the fabric from selvage to selvage.

1. From each fabric, cut two 1½"-wide strips. Make two identical strip-pieced units, using one strip of each fabric in each unit. Use ¼"-wide seam allowances and press all the seam allowances in each unit in one direction. Each strip-pieced unit should measure 6½" x 42" to 44".

2. Using a 45° x 90° right-angle triangle, cut each strip-pieced unit into six triangles for a total of twelve. Rotate the triangle with each cut as shown. Each triangle will measure approximately 8½" on two short sides. See Figure 1.

Note: To get the sixth triangle from the strip-pieced unit it may be necessary to sew the short piece cut from the first end of the unit to the other short end, making sure to match the seams carefully. See Figure 2.

3. Place the triangles on a flat surface and move them around to create a pleasing arrangement. Keep the design symmetrical as shown in Figure 3, or arrange them together in two rows of three blocks each, as shown in the sample below.

4. Sew the long edges of two unlike triangles together, forming squares.

5. Sew the squares together in the desired arrangement. Sew sets of triangles together as required to complete your layout and then sew to the squares. See Figure 4.

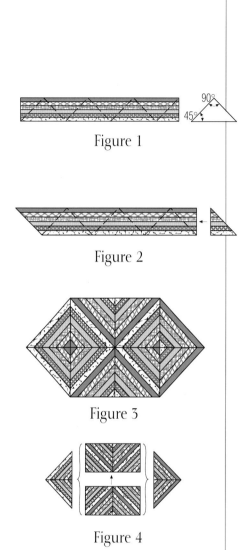

Figure 1

Figure 2

Figure 3

Figure 4

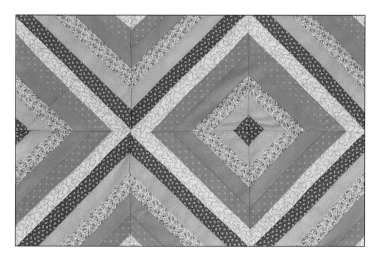

Pieced Squares

This is a very quick technique and the possibilities are endless. You can hide some "uglies" in here!

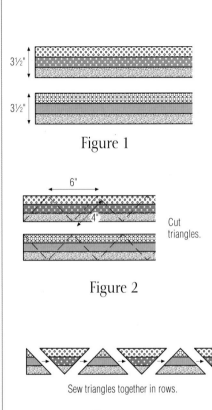

Figure 1

Figure 2

Cut triangles.

Sew triangles together in rows.

Figure 3

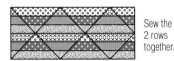

Sew the 2 rows together.

Figure 4

SUPPLIES
1½"-wide strips of five to seven different fabrics

DIRECTIONS
1. Cut a 1½"-wide strip from four different fabrics. From a fifth fabric, cut two 1½"-wide strips. (Strip lengths will vary, depending on the fabric leftovers you have available.)

2. Sew the strips together in two units of 3 strips each, using a strip of the fifth fabric as the last strip in each. See Figure 1. If you wish to cover a larger area with Pieced Squares, use six different fabrics plus a seventh fabric for the ends of each strip-pieced unit.

3. Cut triangles from the strip-pieced units, using a 45° x 90° ruler. Triangles should be 6" long on the long side and 4" long on each of the two short sides. See Figure 2.

4. Sew the triangles together into rows, alternating triangles cut from each strip-pieced unit. Add the partial triangles from the beginning and end of each strip to the ends of the rows. See Figure 3.

5. Sew two rows together so every other triangle forms a square. See Figure 4.

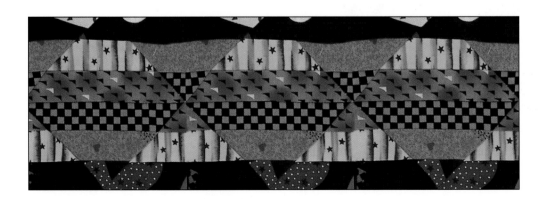

Quick Random Patchwork

Does your quilt need a border? Here's a quickie 6"
border made from eight fabrics used in your quilt.

SUPPLIES
Leftover fabrics

DIRECTIONS

1. Using strips of equal widths that
you already have or that you cut from
leftovers, make a strip-pieced unit. I
used four 2"-wide strips per unit. The
finished unit was 6½" wide. Make a
second unit, using different but coordinating fabrics. See Figure 1.

2. Cut the resulting strip-pieced units
into triangles, using one of your

special rulers—the Kaleidoscope, the
9° Circle Wedge, or the Clearview
Equilateral Triangle, for example. See
Figure 2.

3. Sew the pieces back together, alternating the strip combinations. Use the
strips to cover a desired area, for
instance on a vest front or back.

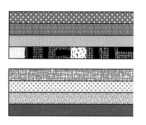

Figure 1

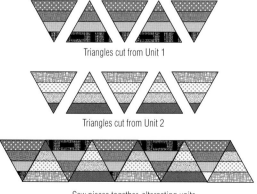

Triangles cut from Unit 1

Triangles cut from Unit 2

Sew pieces together, alternating units.

Figure 2

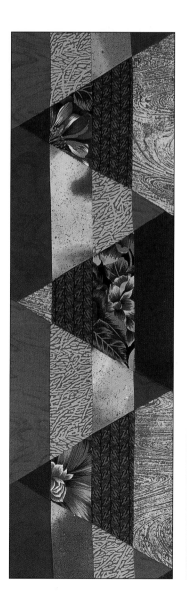

Tricky Triangles

Experiment with the triangle position. You'll be amazed at all the designs you can create!

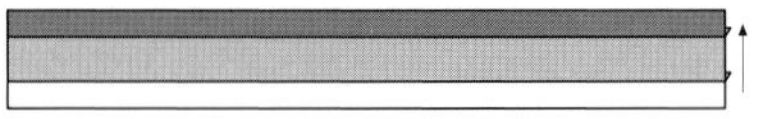

Color Family #1
Make 5 strip-pieced units.

Figure 1

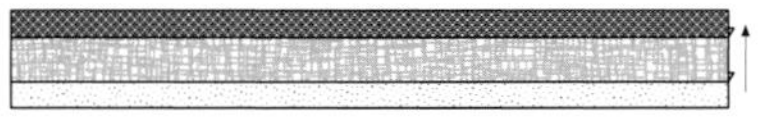

Color Family #2
Make 2 strip-pieced units.

Figure 2

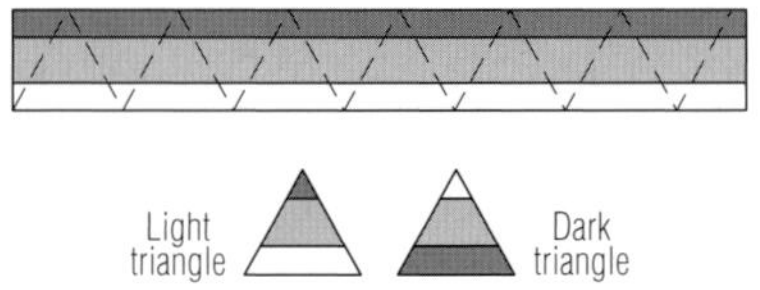

Light triangle   Dark triangle

Figure 3

Horizontal   Vertical

Figure 4

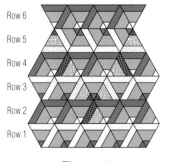

Row 6
Row 5
Row 4
Row 3
Row 2
Row 1

Figure 5

SUPPLIES

Color Family 1 (background color): ⅓ yard each of dark and light fabric, ½ yard of medium fabric

Color Family 2 (accent color): ⅛ yard each of dark and light fabric, ¼ yard of medium fabric

Muslin or other foundation fabric

60° equilateral triangle

DIRECTIONS

Note: Cut all strips across the width of the fabric from selvage to selvage.

1. From Color Family 1, cut five 2"-wide strips of dark, five 3"-wide strips of medium, and five 2"-wide strips of light fabric.

2. Make five identical strip-pieced units, arranging strips as shown. Sew strips together ¼" from the long raw edges. Press the seam allowances toward the darkest strip. See Figure 1.

3. From Color Family 2, cut two 2" wide strips of dark, two 3"-wide strips of medium, and two 2"-wide strips of light fabric.

4. Make two identical strip-pieced units, arranging the strips in each set in the same order as the cutting order above. Sew the strips together ¼" from the long raw edges. Press the seam allowances toward the dark strip in each unit. See Figure 2.

5. Using a 60° equilateral triangle ruler, cut triangles from the strip-pieced units, alternating the direction of the point. You will have dark triangles with dark bases and light triangles with light bases. See Figure 3. From each of the seven strip-pieced units, cut as many triangles as possible. Set aside the partial pieces at the ends of the strips. If necessary, you can piece them together to make a complete triangle.

6. Beginning at the bottom edge of the foundation fabric, arrange the triangles as shown in Figure 4 (or create your own design). To do this, position the triangles in a pleasing arrangement, row by row. Note that the triangles alternate in the rows in horizontal and vertical positions. See Figure 5.

7. When you are pleased with the design you have laid out on top of the foundation, stitch the triangles together, row by row, using ¼"-wide seam allowances and matching seams and raw edges. Press the seam allowances toward one of the triangles in the pair. See Figure 6. Then sew triangle pairs together to complete the rows. Place each completed row in position on the foundation to keep the design rows in place.

8. To sew the rows to the foundation, begin with Row 1 at the bottom and pin it in place. Flip Row 2 down onto Row 1 with right sides together and raw edges even. Pin carefully with seam lines matching. Stitch ¼" from the raw edges. Turn Row 2 up onto the foundation, press, and pin in place. See Figure 7.

9. Sew the remaining rows to the foundation in the same manner, making sure the foundation is smooth and flat underneath.

10. Optional: Using perle cotton or other heavy thread, tack Tricky Triangles to the foundation at each tip of the Color Family 2 triangles. To tack, thread a large-eyed needle with heavy doubled thread. Do not tie in a knot. Take a stitch from the right side through to the back and then back to the right side, taking a ¼" bite. Tie the doubled thread in a double knot on the right side of the patchwork. Clip threads, leaving ½"- to 1"-long tails. See Figure 8.

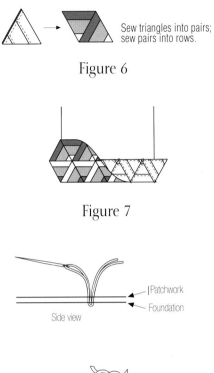

Sew triangles into pairs; sew pairs into rows.

Figure 6

Figure 7

Side view
Patchwork
Foundation

Square Knot

Figure 8

Love and Kisses

This piece is large enough to cover part of a garment or serve as a center medallion in a quilt.

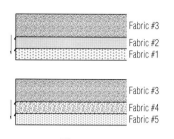

Figure 1

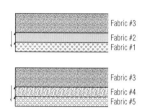

Figure 2

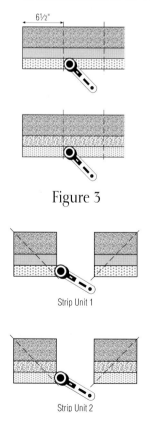

Figure 3

Strip Unit 1

Strip Unit 2

Figure 4

SUPPLIES

One 2" x 42" strip each of Fabrics #1, #2, #4, and #5
Two 3½" x 42" strips of Fabric #3

DIRECTIONS

1. Arrange the strips and sew into Strip Units 1 and 2, making sure to arrange them in the correct sequence. See Figure 1. Use ¼"-wide seam allowances. Press seam allowances in one direction in each unit.

Note: If Fabric #1 or #5 is a directional print, stitch #1 so the design faces up and #5 so the design is upside down in the strip unit. See Figure 2.

2. Crosscut the strip units into 6½" squares. Both strip units should yield six squares. See Figure 3.

3. Stack the squares from Strip Unit 1 in two equal stacks, making sure that Fabric #3 is at the top of each square in each stack. Arrange the stacks side by side. Using a ruler and rotary cutter, cut the stacks diagonally so the cuts form a V from stack to stack as shown. Repeat with the squares from Strip Unit 2. Keep the stacks in this arrangement. See Figure 4.

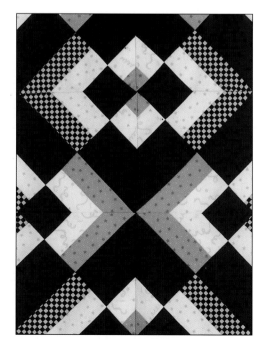

4. Using small pieces of masking tape, label the stacks of triangles as shown. See Figure 5. Remember to remove the labels later.

5. Working from the bottom of each stack so you don't lose the tape labels, arrange all the triangles on a flat surface. See Figure 6. Arrange them into three units.

6. To assemble the units, sew each set of two adjacent triangles together, matching the seams; press the seam allowance in one direction. Sew the remaining two triangles together and press the seam allowance in the opposite direction. Sew the pieced triangles together to complete each square. See Figure 7.

7. Sew the squares together in rows, then sew the rows together, being careful to match the seams at intersections. See Figure 8.

8. You may add decorative buttons where the squares meet in the completed patchwork. Besides adding design interest, they will secure the layers and hide mistakes if the seams don't match perfectly.

Figure 5

Figure 6

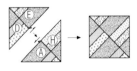

Figure 7

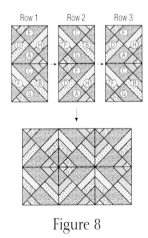

Figure 8

Striking Stripes

Combine this technique with the Striking Stripes Square and use them in one garment for continuity.

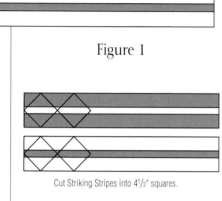

Figure 1

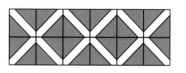

Cut Striking Stripes into 4¹/₂" squares.

Figure 2

Figure 3

SUPPLIES

¼ yard each of two different striped fabrics (A and B)
Muslin or other foundation fabric
Quilter's Rule Jr.

DIRECTIONS

1. Cutting across the fabric width, cut two 3"-wide strips and one 1½"-wide strip from each striped fabric.

2. Sew the narrow strip of one fabric between the wide strips of the other fabric and vice versa, creating two strip-pieced units. See Figure 1. Press the seam allowances away from the center strip in each unit.

3. Using a Quilter's Rule Jr. or other 4½"-square cutting template, place the 45°-line on the center strip and cut the strip-pieced units into 4½" squares. See Figure 2. You will get five to seven squares from each unit (10 to 14 total).

4. Use the squares to create a variety of design rows. When pleased with the arrangement, piece the rows together and press. Pin the completed piece to your foundation and use the triangles left over from cutting the squares to make Striking Stripes Squares. (see opposite). Trim the Striking Stripes even with the edges of the foundation and stitch ¼" from the raw edges. See Figure 3.

Striking Stripes Square

When shopping for a fabric stash, don't overlook the stripes—they make great designs.

SUPPLIES
Leftover triangles from Striking Stripes

DIRECTIONS
1. Arrange four like triangles into a square. See Figure 1.

2. Using a ¼" seam allowance, sew two triangles together to make two halves. See Figure 2.

3. Sew two halves together to make a square. See Figure 3.

4. Repeat Steps 1-3 with remaining triangles to make six blocks.

5. Make two rows of three blocks each, alternating the blocks. Join the rows together, matching the seams.

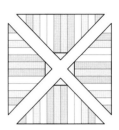

Figure 1

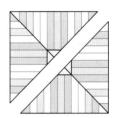

Figure 2

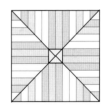

Figure 3

Woven-Square Strips

The dividing solid squares double the amount of patchwork you make from these strips.

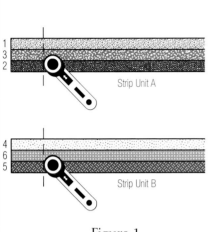

Figure 1

SUPPLIES

1½" x 42" strip each of Fabrics #1, #2, #3, #4, #5, and #6

Two 3½" x 42" strips of Fabric #7

DIRECTIONS

1. Using ¼" seam allowances, sew the fabric strips together in sets of three, making Strip Unit A with Fabrics #1, #2, and #3 and Strip Unit B with Fabrics #4, #5, and #6. Sew the strips together so they go from light to dark in each set. Each strip-pieced unit should measure 3½" x 42". Crosscut each unit into 12 squares, each 3½" x 3½", for a total of 24 squares—12 of A and 12 of B. See Figure 1.

2. From the strips of Fabric #7, cut 19 squares, each 3½" x 3½". These are the C squares in Figure 2. Arrange the squares on a flat surface in the order shown in Figure 2.

3. Using ¼" seam allowances, sew the squares together in rows. Press the seam allowances in opposite directions from row to row. Sew the rows together, matching the seam intersections. See Figure 3.

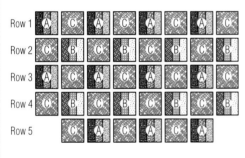

Figure 2

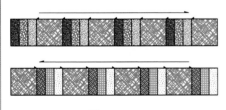

Figure 3

Stepping Stones

You'll be surprised which four-patch blocks appear the most prominent in the completed patchwork.

SUPPLIES
Three 1½" x 42" strips each of four different fabrics (12 strips total)

DIRECTIONS
1. Using ¼" seam allowances, sew four strips together to make a 4½" x 42" strip-pieced unit. Press the seam allowances in one direction. Repeat with the remaining strips, making a total of three identical strip-pieced units. See Figure 1.

2. Cut three 14"-long segments from each strip-pieced unit. (If your strip units are less than 42" long, cut the units into three pieces of equal length.) Sew the segments together to make three identical strip-pieced units. See Figure 2.

3. Working with one unit at a time, cut each strip unit into 1½"-wide segments. You should get eight to ten segments from each unit. Leave the segments in the order they're cut. After you have cut the entire unit into segments, reverse every other strip so unlike blocks are next to each other. See Figure 3.

4. Sew the strips back together again. You should have three identical pieced units. See Figure 4.

5. Sew the units together to make one long piece of patchwork, measuring approximately 12" x 24".

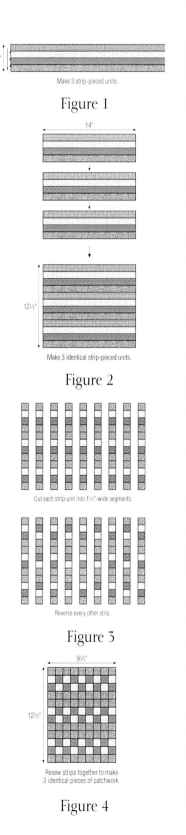

4½"

Make 3 strip-pieced units.

Figure 1

14"

12½"

Make 3 identical strip-pieced units.

Figure 2

Cut each strip unit into 1½"-wide segments.

Reverse every other strip.

Figure 3

9½"

12½"

Resew strips together to make 3 identical pieces of patchwork.

Figure 4

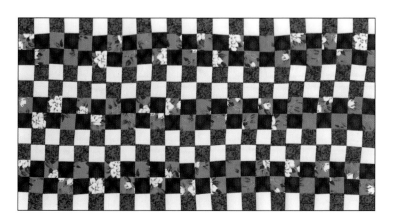

Strip-Pieced Triangle Block

Apply this technique as a filler between blocks or rows of patchwork—it uses lots of leftover and scrap fabrics.

Figure 1

Figure 2

Figure 3

Figure 4

Figure 5

Figure 6

Figure 7

SUPPLIES

Leftovers from other patchwork techniques or ⅔ yard of fabric if you prefer to cut all strips from the same fabric

Scraps of fabric for triangles, which should contrast with the strip fabric(s)

Muslin or other foundation fabric

DIRECTIONS

1. Cut four or more 3⅞" triangles. See Figure 1.

2. From the fabric leftovers, cut several 2"-wide strips of fabric.

3. Pin a triangle to the bottom edge of the foundation. See Figure 2.

4. With right sides together, stitch a 2"-wide strip of fabric to one side of the triangle. Turn the strip toward the foundation and press. Stitch a second strip to the other side of the triangle. See Figure 3. Turn toward the foundation and press. Pin the strip edges to the foundation.

5. Place the ¼" mark of a ruler at the point of the first triangle and draw a line across the strips parallel to the lower edge of the foundation piece. Remove the ruler and trim away the excess on each strip. See Figure 4.

6. With right sides together, pin the long edge of the next triangle to the top of the cut strips. Stitch ¼" from the raw edges. See Figure 5.

7. Turn the triangle up to make sure you didn't stitch across the triangle point. If you did, stitch a narrower seam and remove the first stitching.

   Turn this triangle up onto the foundation and press. See Figure 6. Add strips, press, and trim as before.

8. Continue this process until you have added all the triangles, then continue adding parallel strips until the foundation is covered. See Figure 7. Trim the strip ends even with the foundation piece.

STRIP-PIECING TECHNIQUES
— ROWS OF STRIPS —

Rows of strips work especially well for covering your foundation fabric using the collage method as shown in projects throughout the book.

Jacket Techniques:

The Long and Short of It

A great way to combine bits and pieces of leftover strips from other projects.

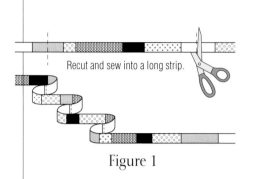

Recut and sew into a long strip.

Figure 1

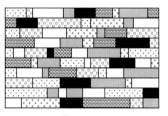

Figure 2

SUPPLIES
1½"-wide strips of fabric—length is not important

DIRECTIONS
1. Toss the strips together and disregard strips that aren't pleasing to the combination.

2. Stitch the 1½"-wide strips together, end to end, to make one long strip. Cut the strip into a variety of lengths. Sew the new lengths together into one very long strip. See Figure 1.

3. Cut this strip into pieces of determined length. Position the strips in a pleasing arrangement. Try not to let like fabrics touch. Sew the strips together, using a ¼"-wide seam allowance. See Figure 2.

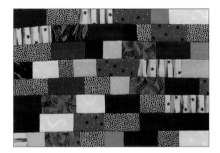

Strip-Stitched Scrappys

Try stitching this no-fail patchwork with decorative thread in the bobbin. You'll enjoy the results.

Figure 1

20"

Figure 2

SUPPLIES
Four different printed fabrics
Piece of muslin or other foundation fabric
Decorative thread or Ribbon Floss for the bobbin

DIRECTIONS
1. From each of four fabrics, cut one 2"-wide strip. Stitch the strips together along the long edges. Press all the seam allowances in one direction. Fold the 6½"-wide strip-pieced unit in half crosswise and cut into two pieces of equal length. See Figure 1.

2. Cut an assortment of 1"- to 2"-wide strips that are the same length as the two strip-pieced units. Arrange the strip-pieced units one above the other and add the assorted strips between, above, and below the units so contrasting fabrics are next to each other. Sew the strips together to make a 20"-wide unit. Press the seam allowances in one direction. See Figure 2.

3. Place the 60° line on a 24"-long ruler even with the top edge of the strip-pieced unit. Make a 60° cut. Using the cut edge as a guide, cut the unit into strips, varying the widths from 1" to no more than 3". See Figure 3.

4. Arrange the strips next to each other, offsetting them and turning some around to create a new design. See Figure 4. Two short pieces can be sewn together to make one long piece. When pleased with the results, stitch the strips together, using ¼"-wide seam allowances. Press the seam allowances in one direction. Pin the unit to a foundation fabric.

5. Cut a ¾"-wide strip of fabric that will show up against the patchwork. From this strip, cut scraps of varying widths, none longer than ½". Cut approximately 30 Scrappys.

6. Position and pin the Scrappys on top of the patchwork in a pattern of your choice. Using a decorative thread in your sewing machine, machine-stitch across the Scrappys to hold them in place.

Note: If you would like to experiment with Ribbon Floss, hand wind it onto a bobbin. When you thread your machine, bypass the tension in the bobbin case if your machine has a drop-in bobbin. If your machine has a bobbin case, purchase an extra bobbin case and loosen the tension screw so the Ribbon Floss slides through easily. Stitch with the foundation side up. You will be stitching "blind" so use the pins holding the Scrappys in place as a guide. Do a test to see if you like the results and experiment with different stitches.

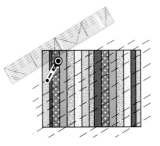

Figure 3

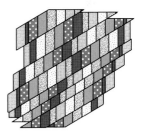

Figure 4

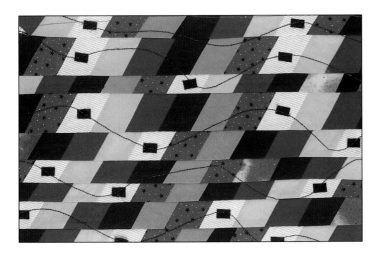

Zigzag Strata

This patchwork can be made effectively striking with a wide variety of fabrics you may have on hand.

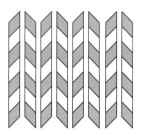

Cut strips at 45° angle.

Right-pointing strips   Left-pointing strips

Figure 1

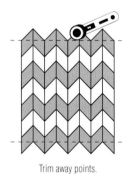

Trim away points.

Figure 3

SUPPLIES
Seven 2" x 42" strips of fabric

DIRECTIONS

1. Alternating contrasting colors and patterns, sew the strips together in a band. Press all the seam allowances in one direction.

2. Fold the strip-pieced unit in half, wrong sides together. Place a ruler with the 45° line parallel to one of the seams and close to the folded edge. Cutting at a 45° angle, cut four 2"-wide strips. You will have a total of eight strips, four angling to the right, and four to the left. Set aside leftover pieces A and B for a future project. See Figure 1.

3. Unstack each set of strips and arrange pairs next to each other to create a zigzag pattern. See Figure 2.

4. Matching the seams at the intersections, sew these strips together. Press the seam allowances in one direction. Using a rotary cutter, trim the top and bottom edges so they are straight. Or, you may choose to leave the zigzag points at one or both edges to overlap, and then appliqué them in place on another fabric.

Figure 2

Chevron Stripes

Let a striped fabric do the work for you when you sew
this impressive patch.

SUPPLIES

⅓ yard of an even-striped fabric
Muslin or other foundation fabric

DIRECTIONS

1. With the fabric folded selvage to
selvage, cut a 10"-wide strip across the
width of the fabric.

2. Without unfolding the strip, cut
the folded end at a 45° angle. Then cut
one 1"-wide strip; two 2"-wide strips;
and one 3"-wide strip. See Figure 1.
Since you cut through two layers of
fabric, you will have a total of eight
strips.

3. Lay out the strips in the arrangement shown, so the stripes form a
chevron where the strip edges meet.
See Figure 2. Stitch the strips together, using ¼"-wide seam allowances.

4. Position a point of the chevron
stripes in the lower corner of your
foundation piece. Trim the bottom
and sides even with the outer edges of
the foundation piece and stitch ¼"
from the raw edges to secure.

5. Using the corner pieces that remain
after cutting the strips from the
striped fabric, cut several pieces to continue the pattern to the left and right
as needed, to cover the foundation
square where it is not covered by the
chevron stripes.

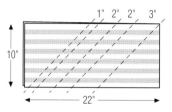

Figure 1

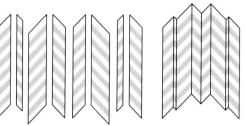

Figure 2

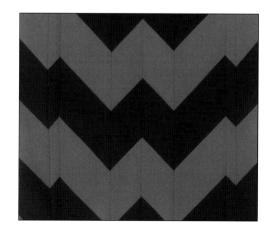

Elinor's Fan

This is a great fill-in block, and can be made in any size you need. It works with many fabrics.

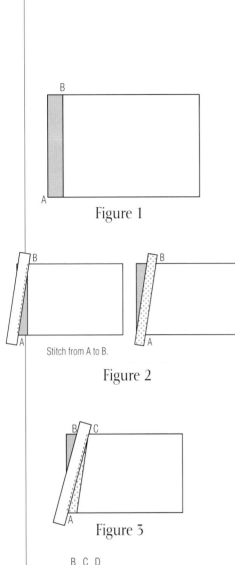

Figure 1

Stitch from A to B.

Figure 2

Figure 3

Figure 4

SUPPLIES

Any size piece of muslin for the foundation fabric
Assorted strips of fabric, cut no wider than 2"

DIRECTIONS

1. Pin a strip of fabric right side up along one short edge of the muslin foundation. Point A is home point. Each strip of fabric you add to create Elinor's Fan must be stitched from this point to the next one (in alphabetical order). See Figure 1.

2. Place the next strip, right side down, partially on the first strip, positioning it from Point A to Point B. Stitch ¼" from the raw edge of the second strip. Trim the first strip even with the stitched raw edge of the second. Finger-press the second strip to the right and pin in place. See Figure 2. Trim the excess at the top and bottom of the second strip even with the edges of the muslin foundation.

3. Position the third strip, right side down, from Point A to Point C. Stitch, trim, press, and pin as described for the second strip. See Figure 3.

4. Repeat this process until the entire muslin piece is covered with strips of varying widths. See Figure 4. Try to keep the muslin foundation free of wrinkles as you stitch on the strips. If small wrinkles do develop, don't worry, but do make sure the strip-pieced fan remains as flat as possible.

STRIP-PIECING TECHNIQUES

— 9° WEDGES —

When I discovered this wedge tool many years ago, I had no idea how often I would use it. It's great for cutting strips into patchwork or for use as a template.

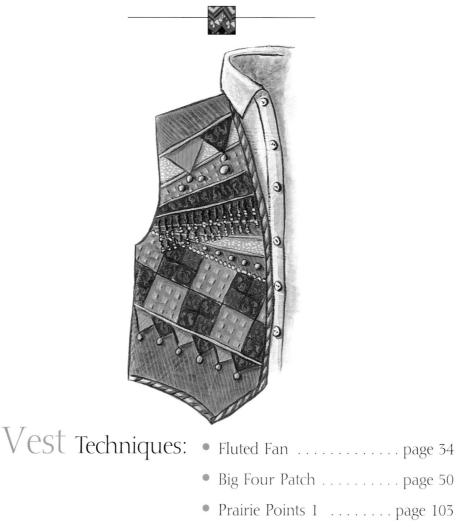

Fandango Fan

How about using these two colorful fans for both sleeves on a fun jacket?

SUPPLIES

Strips cut from 12 fabrics (see
  Step 1, below)
9° Circle Wedge Ruler

DIRECTIONS

Note: Cut all strips across the width of the fabric from selvage to selvage.

1. Cut two strips of each fabric in the width indicated below:
Fabrics #1 and #6: 3" wide
Fabric #2: 1" wide
Fabrics #3 and #8: 2½" wide
Fabrics #4, #5, #10, and #11: 2" wide
Fabrics #7, #9, and #12: 1½" wide

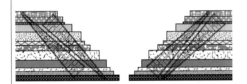

Figure 1

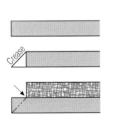

Figure 2

Figure 3

2. Lay out the strips in two identical sets, arranging the strips as desired to create color and value contrast. Use a strip that is an accent color for the center. It is not necessary to keep the strips in numerical order.

3. Sew the strips together to make two staggered opposing sets. Stagger one set to the left and one set to the right; stitch. See Figure 1. To stagger the strips, fold the short end of each strip down to meet the long edge (45° angle), and crease. Open out the corner and place the short end of the next strip at the crease. See Figure 2. Continue staggering in this manner for the first strip set, then stagger from the opposite end for the second strip set. Press the seam allowances up in one set and down in the other set.

4. Using the Circle Wedge Ruler, cut as many wedges as possible from each set. Alternate the ruler position with each cut, making opposite angle cuts. To do this, position the 45° line on the Circle Wedge ruler parallel to a seam line on the stitched sets. Use the same seam line to position the ruler for each new cut.

5. Stack like wedges together. You will have four stacks of four to five wedges each. Of the four stacks, two will have one color at the wide end, and the other two will have another color at the wide end.

6. Arrange the wedges into two chevron fans, placing the wide and narrow ends of mirror-image pairs together. You will create two separate fans. Using ¼"-wide seam allowances, sew together the pieces for each fan. Press the seam allowances in one direction. See Figure 3.

Wonder Wedge

Make a series of these fans to use in the center of a quilt, alternating the fan orientation.

SUPPLIES
⅛ yard each of 13 fabrics
9° Circle Wedge Ruler

DIRECTIONS

1. Cut a strip from each of the 13 fabrics, varying the cut widths from 1" to 3" for interest. Cut each strip across the width of the fabric, selvage to selvage.

2. Arrange strips with like colors together, and blend one color into the next. The two strips in the center of your arrangement will be the most prominent in the finished piece, so plan accordingly.

3. When you are pleased with the arrangement, sew the strips together, using ¼" seam allowances. Press all the seam allowances in one direction. The finished piece should measure approximately 22" x 42".

4. Using the Circle Wedge Ruler, cut as many 60° wedges as possible. Position the wedge-shaped ruler with the wide end up at the top strip of the pieced fabric and with the 60° mark parallel to the seam lines. Cut the first wedge. See Figure 1.

5. Turn the ruler so the wide end is down at the bottom of the last strip, align the 60° mark as before, and cut the next wedge. Continue alternating the direction of the ruler and cutting wedges until you have cut the desired number of wedges. Save the leftover triangles for piecing an additional strip if needed.

Note: The 60° mark will not hit in the same place on the strip-pieced unit for the large end and the small end of the ruler. However, it is important to always line it up in the same location for all cuts made with the wide end up and those made with the short end up. That way, you will have two sets of matching wedges.

6. Sew the wedges together, using ¼" seam allowances and alternating the orientation of the wedges. See Figure 2. It helps to pin the wedges together at the top and bottom of each seam. Press seam allowances in one direction.

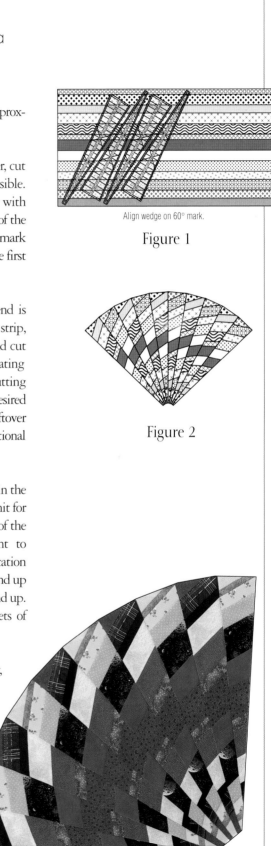

Align wedge on 60° mark.

Figure 1

Figure 2

Fluted Fan

Bright colors and a yard of braid combine into a "fan"-tastic segment for your next garment.

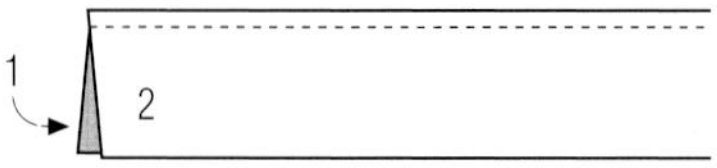

Figure 1

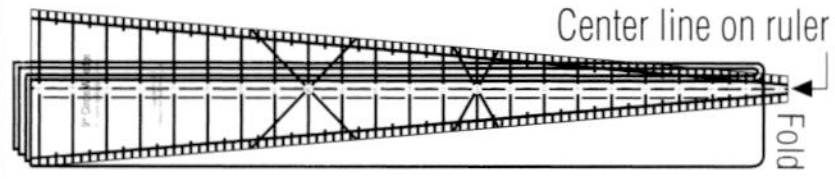

Figure 2

Cut 2 wedge sets from joined strips.

Center line on ruler

Fold

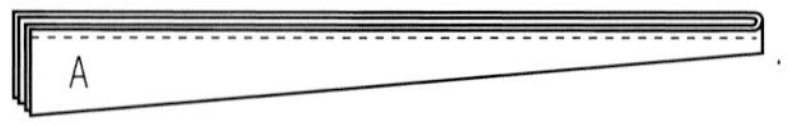

Figure 3

A

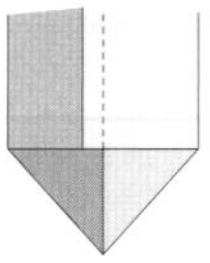

Figure 4

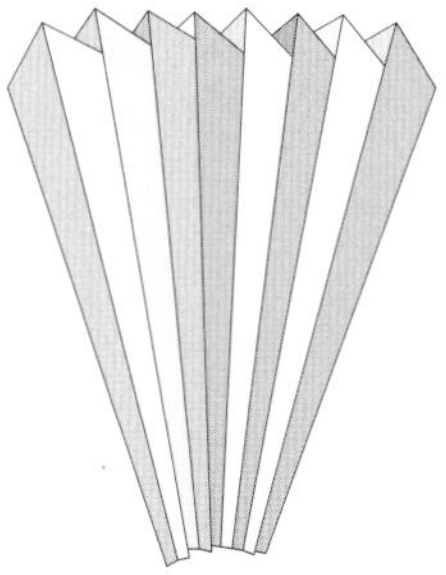

Figure 5

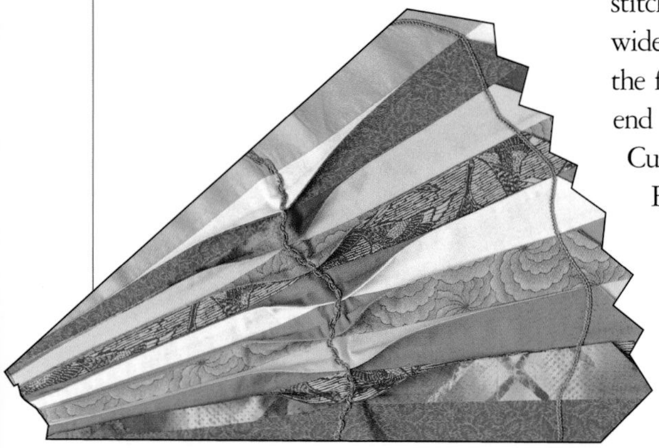

SUPPLIES

⅛ yard each of eight fabrics*
1 yard of braid
9° Circle Wedge Ruler
*Choose four light and four dark fabrics, or choose four fabrics of one color and four of another, such as red and black. One set will be Group 1 and the other Group 2.

DIRECTIONS

1. Cut a 2½"-wide strip from each of the eight fabrics, cutting across the fabric width (crosswise grain).

2. With right sides together, sew a strip from Group 1 to a strip from Group 2, stitching ¼" from the raw edges. Do not press. Repeat with the remaining strips. See Figure 1. You should have four sets of two strips each.

3. Work with one set of strips at a time. With the strips still facing each other in the sewing position, fold the strips in half crosswise. Cut two wedge sets from the folded strip, using the 9° Circle Wedge Ruler. Position the ruler with the center line exactly on the stitching line, making sure that the wide end of the ruler is completely on the fabric. Don't worry if the narrow end extends beyond the fabric fold. Cut along the edge of the ruler. See Figure 2.

4. Cut the resulting piece (A) apart on the fold for two wedge sets. Save the other piece for another project. See Figure 3.

5. With the wedges still folded right sides together, stitch across the wider end ¼" from the raw edges. Clip corners. Finger press the seam allowance to one side. Turn right side out and press with an iron. The piece should look like the point of a man's tie. See Figure 4.

6. Arrange the wedges in a fan formation by placing one wedge on a flat surface so the whole piece shows. Add seven more wedge sets, always placing the first half of each one behind the previous wedge. This will give you an idea of how the piece will look when finished; you will sew the wedges together and then pleat to create the "fluted" effect. See Figure 5.

7. With raw edges even and right sides together, stitch the wedges together to make one big fan. Press all seam allowances in one direction.

8. Place the fan on a flat surface. Starting with the second set of wedges, fold the first wedge in each set in half down the center and press. The entire point of each wedge should still show when the pleating is completed. Pin. Stitch the folds in place across the small end of the fan.

9. Stitch 1" below the fan points to hold them in place and add cross-locked beads or braid. In the middle of the fan, open the fold of each wedge to reveal the inside pair and pin in place. Then stitch braid on top.

STRIP-PIECING TECHNIQUES

— BARGELLO —

Bargello is a great technique to use for a large area such as the back of a garment or the main body of a quilt. It was derived from the long and short stitches used in needlepoint.

Apron Techniques:

Rhapsody Bargello

Yes, there are ¾"-wide strips used in this technique! It's possible though, with a very interesting effect.

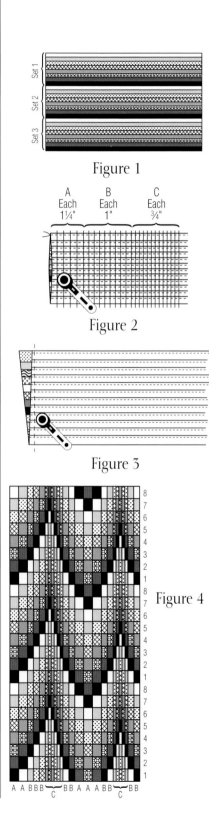

Figure 1

Figure 2

Figure 3

Figure 4

SUPPLIES
¼ yard each of eight fabrics

DIRECTIONS

1. Choose one of the eight fabrics as the accent color (#1). This is the black strip in each set in Figure 1. Plan the arrangement of the remaining fabrics so the colors blend in a natural progression. Assign them numbers 2–8.

2. Cut three 1½"-wide strips from each of the eight fabrics. Cut all strips across the fabric width. You should have a total of 24 strips.

3. Sew the strips together in numerical order, using ¼" seam allowances. Make three identical units, pressing all the seam allowances toward the accent fabric, then sew the three units together. See Figure 1. The finished piece should measure 24" x 40".

4. With right sides together, sew the first and last strip together to make a tube; press the seam allowance in the same direction as all the others. Using your rotary-cutting equipment and referring to Figure 2, cut the tube into the following strips, or rings: five 1¼"-wide strips (A), nine 1"-wide strips (B), and eleven ¾"-wide strips (C). Cut 1½"-wide strips from any remaining tube.

Note: The strip-pieced tube should lie flat when folded in half in preparation for stitching. If it does not, stitch from the center out, stitching as far as it lies flat. Cut only as many strips as possible before you need to realign and

stitch more of the tube. Each time you cut a new series of strips, first cut a new straight edge on the tube. See Figure 3.

5. Referring to Figure 3, lay out the rings as follows: two As, three Bs, six Cs, two Bs, three As, two Bs, five Cs, and two Bs.

Open each ring at the correct location to create the strip layout by tugging gently at each end of the seam to loosen the stitches. In Figure 4, the black segments are the accent color. Add the 1½"-wide strips to the right and left sides as desired.

6. Sew the strips together, using scant ¼" seam allowances. It is not necessary to pin the strips together; just hold them together while you sew, matching each seam line by pulling gently or releasing the fabric strips. (Remember, this is recreational sewing. If seams don't match perfectly, it doesn't matter!)

Symmetrical Bargello

This makes a piece large enough to cover the back of a jacket or vest.

SUPPLIES
¼ yard each of eight fabrics

DIRECTIONS

1. Cut three 1½"-wide strips from each of the eight fabrics. Cut all strips across the fabric width. Assign each fabric a number and sew the strips together in numerical order, using ¼" seam allowances. Press all the seam allowances in one direction. The finished unit will have three sets of strips seamed together and should measure approximately 24" x 42". See Figure 1.

2. Fold the strip-pieced unit in half, right sides together, with the raw edges of the first and last strips matching. Stitch ¼" from the edge to make one long tube. See Figure 2.

Note: The strip-pieced tube should lie flat when folded in half in preparation for stitching. If it does not, stitch from the center out, only as far as it lies flat. Cut strips from the stitched section of the tube as directed in Step 3. Cut only as many as possible until you need to realign the raw edges and stitch more of the tube. Before cutting each new series of strips, first cut a new straight edge on the tube.

3. Using your rotary-cutting equipment, cut the tube into rings. Make the first one 1" wide. Then cut two each of the following widths: 1¼", 1½", 1¾", 2", and 2¼". Continue to cut strips in sets of two, increasing the width by ¼" each time, until you can no longer cut two of a given width. See Figure 3. (Strip-piecing seams are not shown in Figure 3 for the sake of clarity.)

4. Open one seam of the 1"-wide strip at any seam line by tugging gently at each side to loosen the stitches. Place right side up on a flat surface with the seam allowances pressed toward you. This strip will be the center of the Bargello.

5. Identify the top fabric of the 1"-wide strip. Find this same fabric in the two 1¼"-wide strips; open these strips one segment down from the fabric you identified, making sure that the seam allowances are still pressed toward you. The second fabric in the 1"-wide strip should be at the top of the 1¼"-wide strips. Position a strip at each side of the center strip, with top edges even. See Figure 4.

6. Repeat Step 5 with each remaining set of strips, moving down one segment each time you open the seam of a new strip. Face all seam allowances toward you. Double-check to make sure the design is symmetrical on each side of the center strip.

7. Pick up and stack the strips one at a time, in order. Place a pin in the top left corner of the top strip to remind yourself not to sew to that edge.

8. Stitch the strips in order, using ¼" seam allowances. There is no need to match the patchwork; simply manipulate it to make the seams match the best you can. Your eye will see the design, not the accuracy in piecing.

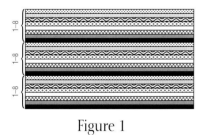

Figure 1

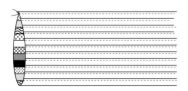

Figure 2

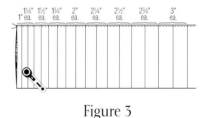

Figure 3

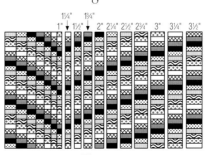

Figure 4

Woven Bargello

Just concentrate, and these long and short woven strips are easy to make with strip piecing.

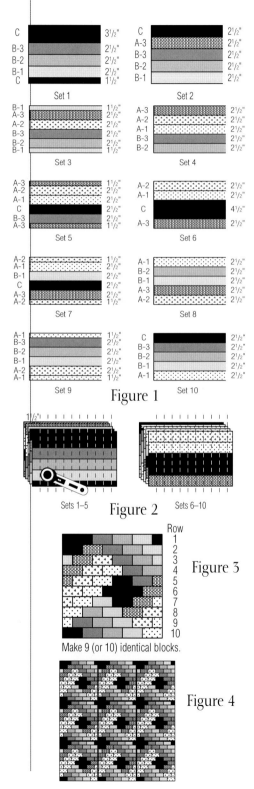

Figure 1

Figure 2

Sets 1–5   Sets 6–10

Figure 3

Row
1
2
3
4
5
6
7
8
9
10

Make 9 (or 10) identical blocks.

Figure 4

SUPPLIES

½ yard each of Fabrics A-1, A-2, and A-3 for set 1*
½ yard each of Fabrics B-1, B-2, and B-3 for set 2*
½ yard of contrast Fabric C
*Choose two sets of blending fabrics, such as gradations of purple and green.

CUTTING CHART

Fabric A-1	Two strips	1½" x 16"
	Six strips	2½" x 16"
Fabric A-2	Two strips	1½" x 16"
	Six strips	2½" x 16"
Fabric A-3	Two strips	1½" x 16"
	Six strips	2½" x 16"
Fabric B-1	Two strips	1½" x 16"
	Six strips	2½" x 16"
Fabric B-2	Seven strips	2½" x 16"
Fabric B-3	Seven strips	2½" x 16"
Fabric C	One strip	4½" x 16"
	One strip	3½" x 16"
	Four strips	2½" x 16"
	Six strips	1½" x 16"

Set the remaining fabric aside.

DIRECTIONS

1. Arrange and sew the strips together into ten 10½" x 16" sets, using ¼"-wide seam allowances. See Figure 1. Press all seam allowances toward the first, top, strip in each set. Pin or tape a tag to the first strip of each set to identify the set by number.

2. Layer together Sets 1–5 and Sets 6–10. Using a rotary cutter and ruler, trim the short left edge of each stack so it is straight and perpendicular to the long edge. Keeping the sets layered, cut ten 1½" strips. See Figure 2.

3. Divide the strips into ten stacks of 1½"-wide strips. Each stack should contain one strip from each set, layered in numerical order. From here on, the set numbers become row numbers.

4. Lay out the strips from one stack in numerical order. Refer to Figure 3 for accuracy of placement. Stitch them together, using ¼" seam allowances. The seams will not match from row to row, but make sure all seam allowances on each strip are pressed in the same direction (check before stitching). Repeat with the remaining stacks. You should have identical blocks.

5. Arrange nine blocks with three rows across and three rows down, placing Row 1 in each block at the top edge of each horizontal row. See Figure 4. Set the remaining block aside to use in another project.

STRIP-PIECING TECHNIQUES
— SEMINOLE WORK —

Seminole is a great piecing method for a beginner to try. It takes very little effort to achieve impressive results. Stretch the area it will cover by adding border strips between Seminole rows.

Pillow Techniques:

Seminole Strip

Add rows of solid fabric between rows of Seminole strips to define each patchwork block.

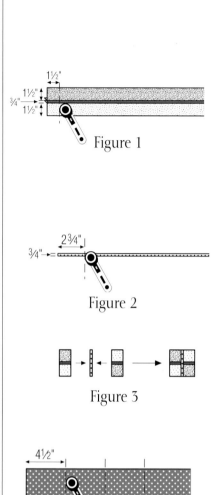

Figure 1

Figure 2

Figure 3

Figure 4

SUPPLIES

1½" x 42" strips each of Fabrics #1 and #2
Two ¾" x 42" strips of Fabric #3
Two 2¾" x 42" strips of Fabric #4

DIRECTIONS

Note: Select four different fabrics that coordinate as well as contrast with each other. Cut a 1½"-wide strip from each of Fabrics #1 and #2. From Fabric #3, cut two strips, each ¾" wide. From Fabric #4, cut two strips, each 2¾" wide.

2. Make a strip-pieced unit with one of the ¾"-wide strips between two of the 1½"-wide strips. Use a ¼"-wide seam allowance and press the seam allowances in one direction. Save the other strips for another step. See Figure 1.

3. Crosscut the entire strip-pieced unit into 1½"-wide segments. See Figure 1.

4. Cut the remaining ¾"-wide strip into 2¾" segments. See Figure 2.

5. Join two of the units cut in Step 2 above with a ¾" x 2¾" segment, reversing the direction of the second strip-pieced unit as shown. See Figure 3. Be sure the ¾" strips line up across from each other. Make as many units as possible from the pieces you have.

6. Cut the 2¾"-wide strips into 4½" segments. See Figure 4.

7. Sew a patchwork unit from Step 5 between every 2¾" x 4½" segment, beginning and and ending with 4½" rectangles. See Figure 5.

8. Cut the resulting strip into parallelograms, placing the ruler ½" from the seam between each rectangle and patchwork unit as shown. See Figure 6.

9. Sew the resulting pieces together, offsetting each strip so the points of the pieced squares line up. As you sew the segments together, determine how many segments you need in a row to cover the desired area. You may use these pieces in vertical or horizontal rows. Trim each long edge, leaving a ¼"-wide seam allowance beyond the points of the pieced squares. See Figure 7.

10. Add the leftover ends at the beginning and end of the stitched strip from Step 8 to the end of the finished strip. Trim the edges even, making sure to leave a seam allowance.

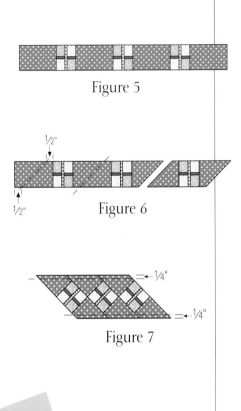

Figure 5

Figure 6

Figure 7

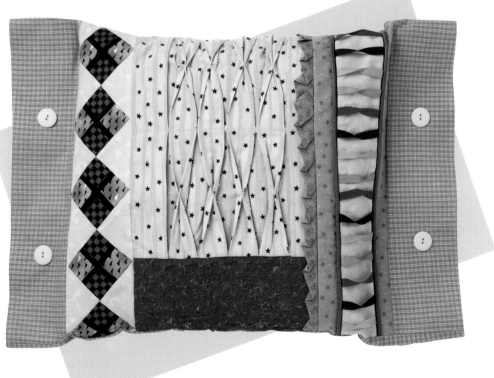

Four-Patch Seminole Patchwork

This is much easier to make than you'd think by looking at the actual patch. Try it!

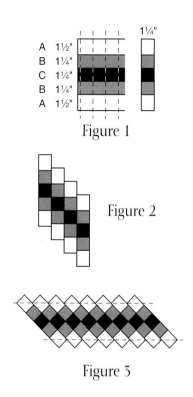

A	1½"
B	1¼"
C	1¼"
B	1¼"
A	1½"

1¼"

Figure 1

Figure 2

Figure 3

Figure 4

SUPPLIES
⅛ yard each of Fabrics #1, #2, and #3

DIRECTIONS

1. Cut the following strips from the three fabrics selected for this patchwork piece, cutting each strip across the fabric width:

    Fabric #1: Two 1½"-wide strips
    Fabric #2: Two 1¼"-wide strips
    Fabric #2: One 1¼"-wide strip

2. With right sides together and using ¼" seam allowances, sew the strips together and press all seams in one direction. The finished piece should measure approximately 5" x 42". Cut the strip-pieced unit into 1¼"-wide strips. See Figure 1.

3. Using a ¼" seam allowance, sew the strips together, offsetting each strip by one square. See Figure 2.

4. Using a rotary cutter and ruler, cut off the points (often called "rooftops" in my classes) on both jagged edges so a ¼" seam allowance remains beyond the corners of each square. See Figure 3.

5. With right sides together, sew the short ends of the Seminole strip together to make a tube. Press the seam allowance in the same direction as all the others. See Figure 4.

6. Make a straight cut through one layer of the tube, opening the piece into one continuous patchwork strip. See Figure 5.

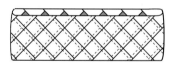

Cut through one layer of tube only.

Figure 5

Simple Seminole Patchwork

This makes a great dividing band for a quilt or wearable.

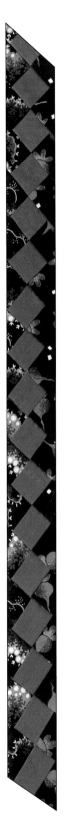

SUPPLIES
One 1½" x 29" strip each of
   Fabrics #1 and #3
One 1¼" x 29" strip of Fabric
   #2

DIRECTIONS
1. Sew the 1¼" strip in between the two 1½" strips, using ¼" seam allowances. Press the seam allowances toward the darker fabric. Cross-cut the unit into 1¼"-wide segments. See Figure 1.

2. Sew the segments together, offsetting each piece by one square and using ¼" seam allowances. Trim away the peaks along the top and bottom edges as shown, making sure ¼" seam allowances remain above and below the inner tip of the center row of squares. See Figure 2.

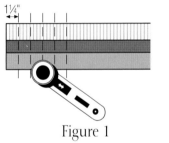

Figure 1

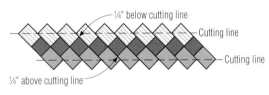

¼" below cutting line
Cutting line
Cutting line
¼" above cutting line

Figure 2

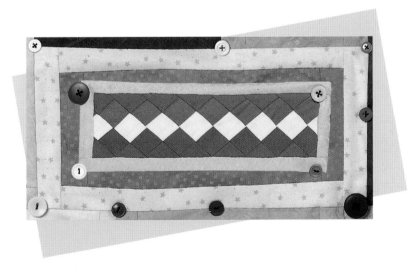

Seminole Stroll

Effort in applying this piecing technique yields eye-catching results.

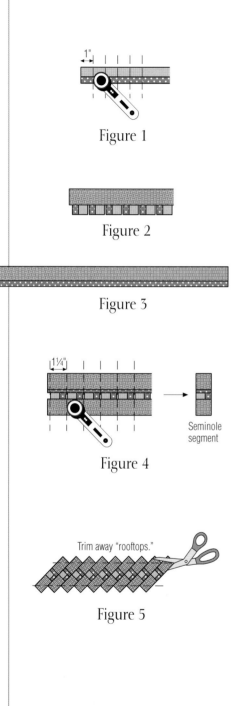

Figure 1

Figure 2

Figure 3

Figure 4

Seminole segment

Trim away "rooftops."

Figure 5

SUPPLIES

Two ¾"-wide strips of Fabric #1
Two 1½"-wide strips of Fabric #2
One 1"-wide strip of Fabric #3

DIRECTIONS

Note: Cut all the strips across the width of the fabric from selvage to selvage.

1. Using a ¼" seam allowance, sew the Fabric #3 strip to a Fabric #1 strip. Press the seam allowance toward the darker fabric. Crosscut the strip-pieced unit into 1"-wide segments. See Figure 1.

2. Stitch a short end of each 1" segment cut in Step 1 to a 1½"-wide strip of Fabric #2. The segment edges should just touch each other without overlapping. Press the seam allowances toward the strip-pieced segments. See Figure 2.

3. Stitch the remaining strip of Fabric #1 to the remaining strip of Fabric #2. Press the seam allowance toward the darker fabric. See Figure 3.

4. Sew the resulting unit to the other edges of the 1" segments as shown. Press the seam allowance toward the strip-pieced unit. Cut into 1¼" segments, cutting between the 1" segments. See Figure 4.

5. Offset the segments by one center square, and chain-stitch together in pairs. Then chain-stitch the pairs together. Continue chain-stitching all units together to create a finished piece that measures approximately 42" long. Trim away and discard the "rooftops," cutting ¼" from the corners of the top and bottom squares in the strips. You may want to mark a cutting line first, and then use your scissors to cut on the line. I find this more accurate than using a rotary cutter for this step. See Figure 5.

TRADITIONAL TECHNIQUES

These techniques are the foundation for all that I do in my design work. It's important to learn and study these techniques and use them as starting points for more and more ideas.

Chair Cover Techniques:

Drunkard's Path

Use the blocks in a border on a quilt or garment, or arrange the 24 blocks to form the basis for a mini quilt.

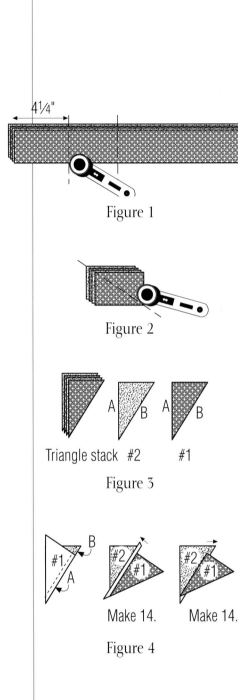

4¼"

Figure 1

Figure 2

Triangle stack   #2   #1

Figure 3

#1   B   A

#2   #1

#2   #1

Make 14.   Make 14.

Figure 4

SUPPLIES
½ yard of Fabric #1
¼ yard each of Fabrics #2
    and #3

DIRECTIONS
Note: Cut all strips across the width of each fabric, from selvage to selvage.

1. From Fabric #1, cut three 4½"-wide background strips. Set aside for Step 8, opposite.

2. For the fan wedges, cut two 2¾"-wide strips each from Fabrics #2 and #3. Open out the strips and layer them in alternating sequence with right sides facing up.

3. Crosscut the stacked strips into 2¾" x 4¼" rectangles. See Figure 1.

4. Cut the rectangles diagonally from the upper left corner to the lower right corner. Be sure to make all cuts in this direction. See Figure 2.

5. Make one stack of all the resulting triangle stacks, making sure all triangles face right side up.

6. Remove the first triangle from the stack and move it to the right. Remove the next triangle and place it between the first triangle and the stack. See Figure 3.

Flip the first triangle over onto the right side of the second triangle, aligning edge A of the first triangle with edge B of the second triangle. Stitch ¼" from the raw edge. See Figure 4.

Make a total of 28 sets of triangles in this manner, chain-sewing to make quick work of this step. In one set of 14, finger-press the seams toward the left-hand triangle in each pair. In the remaining set, finger-press the seam toward the right-hand triangle.

7. Add a third triangle to 14 of the 28 sets in the same manner, creating 14 wedges, each made of three triangles. The two outer triangles in each wedge should be Fabric #2 and the center one should be Fabric #3. Repeat with the remaining 14 sets. The two outer triangles in these wedges should be Fabric #3 and the center one should be Fabric #2. See Figure 5.

8. Using the 4" Drunkard's Path templates (#QR-401 from Quilter's Rule, Inc.) or the templates below, cut 28 concave units (Template B) from the 4½" background fabric strips.

Note: It is easier to cut the concave curves using the rotary cutter with the smaller blade. See Figure 6. Save the teardrop shapes that are left over. They can be appliquéd onto another fabric.

9. Cut 28 convex units (Template A) from the units, being careful to center the template's point in the center triangle in each wedge. See Figure 7.

10. With right sides together, pin each piece A to a piece B, matching the outer edges and the centers. With A on the bottom, stitch ¼" from the raw edges, stitching slowly and smoothing out B to avoid puckers. Press the seam allowance toward B. You should have 28 blocks. See Figure 8. Stitch a row of blocks together in the position of your choice, forming a pleasing pattern.

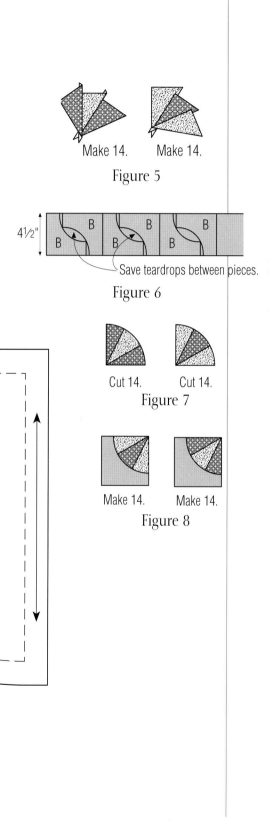

Make 14.   Make 14.

Figure 5

4½"   B   B   B

B   B   B

Save teardrops between pieces.

Figure 6

Cut 14.   Cut 14.

Figure 7

Make 14.   Make 14.

Figure 8

¼" seam allowance

DRUNKARD'S PATH TEMPLATE A

straight of grain

DRUNKARD'S PATH TEMPLATE B

Flying Geese

Use as a dividing strip on a medallion quilt or as a cuff on the sleeve of a jacket.

Figure 1

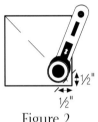

Figure 2

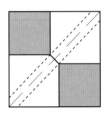

Figure 3

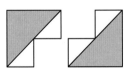

Figure 4

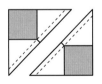

Figure 5

SUPPLIES

¼ yard of fabric for the background

¼ yard of fabric for the flying-geese triangles

DIRECTIONS

1. Cut two 2⅞" strips from the background fabric. From these strips, cut sixteen 2⅞" background squares. Cut a 5¼"-wide strip from the flying-geese fabric, cutting across the width of the fabric. Cut four 5¼" squares from the strip.

Note: Each of the four squares can be cut from a different fabric if you prefer a variety of geese fabrics.

2. On the wrong side of the background squares, draw a diagonal line from one corner to the opposite corner. See Figure 1.

3. Stack the squares in groups of five or six with the marked lines all in the same direction. Cut off a ½" triangle tip on one end as shown, being sure to make this cut across one of the corners that is intersected by the diagonal line. See Figure 2.

4. Position two small squares on top of one large flying-geese square, with right sides together and the cut corner edges facing each other in the center. Machine-stitch ¼" to the left and right of the diagonal line. See Figure 3.

Note: To chain-piece, stitch on one side of the diagonal line on all four squares, then lift the presser foot and, without cutting the threads, turn the pieces and stitch on the opposite side of the line on all four squares. This saves time and thread.

5. Cut the stitched unit in half on the diagonal line. See Figure 4.

6. Press the resulting small background triangles away from the main triangle in each unit. See Figure 5.

7. Now place one background square on each of these units, with right sides together and with the cut corner edge overlapping the center seam line. Stitch ¼" to the left and right of the diagonal line. See Figure 6. To save time, chain-piece the units.

8. Cut the stitched unit in half on the diagonal line, and press the small triangles away from the large triangle. See Figure 7. This yields two flying-geese units per unit, for a total of 16.

9. With right sides together, stitch the flying-geese units together in two rows of eight, using ¼" seam allowances. As you stitch, be careful not to catch the tips of the large triangles in the seams. See Figure 8.

10. Sew the bottom ends of the two strips together. See Figure 9. If you prefer, you may sew the strips together so the "geese" all fly in the same direction.

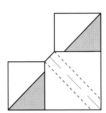

Figure 6

Figure 7

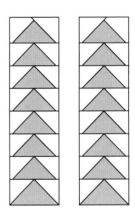

Figure 8

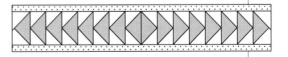

Figure 9

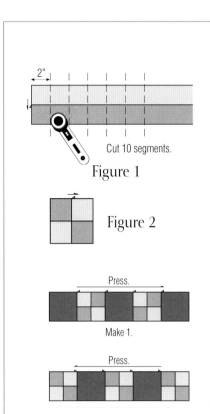

Cut 10 segments.

Figure 1

Figure 2

Press.

Make 1.

Press.

Figure 3

Big Four Patch

To make a larger piece for a quilt or borders, repeat the steps, using another set of accent fabrics.

SUPPLIES
2" x 22" strip each of Fabrics
   #1 and #2
3½" x 42" strip of Fabric #3

DIRECTIONS
1. Sew strips #1 and #2 with right sides together along one long edge, using a ¼"-wide seam allowance. Open the fabric, and press the seam allowance toward the darker fabric. Crosscut the strip into ten 2"-wide segments. See Figure 1.

2. Arrange the segments in four-patch squares and sew together, matching the seams. Press. See Figure 2.

3. From Fabric #3, cut five 3½" squares. Alternate the four-patch squares with the plain squares in two rows of five squares each and sew together; press the seam allowances in opposite directions from row to row. Sew the rows together, alternating the plain squares. See Figure 3.

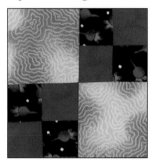

Four-Patch Reverse

A great way to use up scrap-fabric strips. Use only two colorways, or use many colors for a really scrappy look.

SUPPLIES
1½" to 3"-wide strips of several
   fabrics

DIRECTIONS
1. Sew two strips of equal width together along one long edge. Press the seam allowance toward the darker of the two strips. Repeat with the remaining strips.

   Crosscut the strip-pieced unit into sections the same width as the cut width of the individual strips. For example, if you used 2"-wide strips, cut the section 2" wide. See Figure 1.

2. Sew two sections together to create a four-patch block. See Figure 2.

3. Sew the patches together in rows, then sew the rows together to make a piece of patchwork large enough to cover the desired area. See Figure 3.

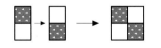

Figure 1

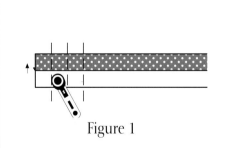

Figure 2

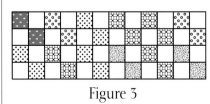

Figure 3

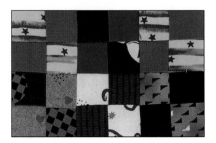

Folded Triangle

Use two patches to make a faced pocket. A button can be added at each point for embellishment.

SUPPLIES
Fabric scraps

DIRECTIONS

1. Cut two 3" squares of one fabric for the background. Cut a 3" x 5½" rectangle of another fabric for the triangle.

2. Fold the rectangle in half wrong sides together, holding the fold at the bottom. With right sides together and all four raw edges even at the top, sandwich the folded rectangle between the squares.

3. Sew the four layers together along the right edge of the stack—don't sew along the top edge! Clip the fold in the seam allowance to the stitching.

4. Open the background squares. Push the folded rectangle to one side. Press the seam allowances open.

5. On the right side, pull the folded rectangle open and bring the raw edge evenly to the top corners, forming a triangle. It's magical! Pin in place.

6. Follow the above instructions to make a second folded-triangle unit, using the same or different fabrics. Sew the folded triangle blocks together along one long edge, catching the raw edge of one triangle in the seam and being careful not to catch the point of the other triangle in the seam. Repeat to make as many units as needed.

Pieced Fans

As a variation, cut along one long edge only and use on the hemline of a skirt or as a final border on a quilt.

SUPPLIES
Fabric scraps
Template plastic

DIRECTIONS

1. Trace the fan pattern on page 58 to make a cutting template. Cut fans from the fabric scraps and arrange them in a pleasing order, alternating the direction of each fan and balancing pattern as well as color.

2. Sew the fans together, using ¼" seam allowances. See Figure 1. Press the seam allowances in one direction.

3. Using a rotary cutter and ruler, trim the long edges of the strip. See Figure 2.

Figure 1

Figure 2

Kaleidoscope Radiance

To create a wall quilt with great visual impact, try adding a border made with Kaleidoscope blocks.

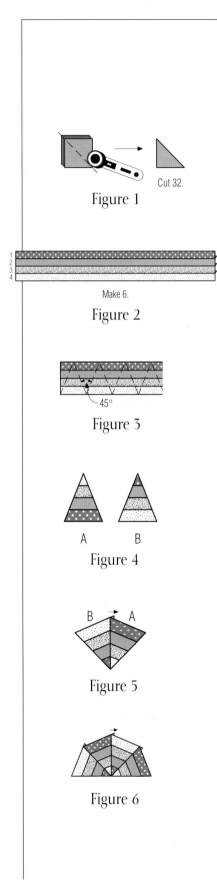

Figure 1

Cut 32.

Press

Make 6.

Figure 2

45°

Figure 3

A   B

Figure 4

B ↗ A

Figure 5

Figure 6

SUPPLIES

⅔ yard each of four different
    Fabrics: #1, very dark;
    #2, medium dark;
    #3, medium light;
    and #4, contrast
45° Kaleidoscope Wedge Ruler

DIRECTIONS

Note: Cut all the strips across the width of the fabric, from selvage to selvage.

1. From each of the four fabrics, cut six 2"-wide strips. You will have a total of 24 strips.

2. From Fabric #2 and Fabric #3, cut eight 4½" squares, for a total of 16 squares. Stack the squares in groups of three or four and cut once diagonally for a total of 32 triangles to use for the corners in Blocks A and B. See Figure 1. Set aside for Step 9.

3. Using strips cut in Step 1, make six identical strip-pieced units. Arrange the strips in numerical order and stitch together ¼" from the long edges. Press the seams toward the darkest strip. Each unit should measure about 6½" x 42". See Figure 2.

4. Use the 6½" marking on the 45° Kaleidoscope Wedge Ruler to cut 14 to 15 wedges from each of the strip units. Cut with the wedge point up and then with the point down, alternating until you can no longer cut a triangle from the strip unit. You will need a total of 72 wedges.

As you position the ruler and cut, make sure the seam lines are parallel to the horizontal lines on the ruler. See Figure 3.

Note: If the fabric seams are not running parallel to the ruler lines, adjust the ruler and make a small cut in your fabric to re-establish the perfect wedge.

5. Divide the wedges into two stacks, placing those with Fabric #1 at the wide end in Stack A (dark wedges) and those with Fabric #4 at the wide end in Stack B (light wedges). See Figure 4.

6. Sew the light and dark wedges together in pairs, chain sewing to make quick work of it (see note below). Always place the light wedge on the bottom and the dark wedge on top with right sides together and seam lines matching. Because you pressed all seam allowances toward the darkest strip in each strip unit, the seams should butt for a perfect match, eliminating the need for much pinning. Stitch from the wide end to the point; press the seam allowances toward the dark wedge. See Figure 5.

Note: Chain piecing saves time and thread. Instead of stopping the machine, lifting the presser foot, and cutting the thread after sewing two pieces together, place another pair just in front of the previous pair and continue stitching. Clip the pairs apart, then chain-sew the pairs together in groups of four in the same manner.

7. Sew the pairs together to create half-blocks in the same manner. Press all seams in the same direction. Trim points that extend beyond the outer edge of the half-blocks. See Figure 6.

8. Sew the half-blocks together in pairs to create nine octagonal blocks, making sure that the seams match at the center and that the outer ends of the wedges match. Stitch from the center out, then flip the piece over and stitch from the center to the opposite end. Press the seam allowances in the same direction as all the others. There will be a slight twist in the center. Press each block flat from the right side. See Figure 7.

9. Divide the blocks into two stacks of four blocks each and set the remaining block aside. Rotate the first stack so that the dark-ended wedges are at the center on all four sides as shown for Block A. Add a dark triangle (cut in Step 2) to the four light-wedge ends of each octagon to create square blocks. Position the second stack of blocks so the light-ended wedges are at the center on all four sides and sew light triangles to the dark corner wedges as shown for Block B. See Figure 8.

Note: If you make another piece of Kaleidoscope Radiance patchwork for another project, consider using two different medium value fabrics for the corners instead of light and dark for a different look.

10. Before you sew the completetd blocks together to complete the patchwork piece, decide whether you want dark or light points at the bottom of your project. For light corners, sew the triangles from Fabric #3 (Step 2) to the dark wedge ends of the remaining block. See Figure 9.

For dark corners, sew the triangles from Fabric #2 (Step 2) to the light wedge ends of the remaining block.

11. Arrange the blocks into three rows of three blocks each, alternating Blocks A and B. See Figure 9.

12. Sew the blocks together in rows, matching seams and pinning to secure for stitching. Press the seam allowances in opposite directions row to row. Then sew the rows together, matching the seams carefully. Press the seam allowances in one direction, then press the completed piece of patchwork smooth and flat.

Note: This design was adapted with permission from Marilyn Doheny's Cutting Edge Quilt Designs as found on the Kaleidoscope Wedge Ruler package.

Make 9.

Figure 7

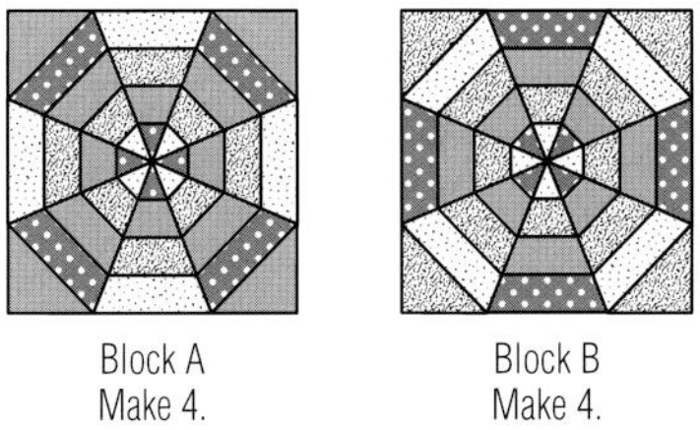

Block A
Make 4.

Block B
Make 4.

Figure 8

Figure 9

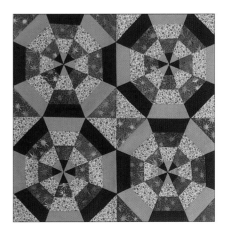

Trip Around the World

Repeat the instructions to make a second patchwork. Join the pieces for a complete Trip Around the World.

Cut 13 from each stack of 3.

Figure 1

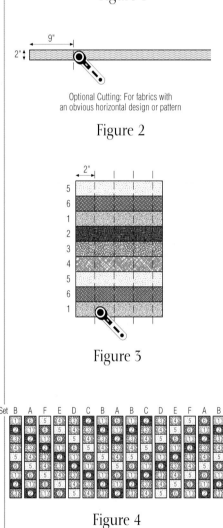

Optional Cutting: For fabrics with an obvious horizontal design or pattern

Figure 2

Figure 3

Figure 4

SUPPLIES

¼ yard each of six different fabrics (Fabrics #1 – #6)

DIRECTIONS

1. Open out the fabrics and layer them in two stacks of three pieces each. Make sure the cut edges are lined up and all wrinkles are smoothed out. Trim away the selvages at one end of each stack, then crosscut 13 strips, each 2" x 9", from the layered fabrics. See Figure 1. You should have a total of 78 strips. The strips are 1" longer than you actually need, to allow for trimming after you sew the sets together.

Note: If one of your fabrics has a directional print that follows a horizontal line, cut three 2"-wide strips across the fabric width (crosswise grain). Cut a total of 12 strips, each 2" x 9", from the strips. Cut one more 2" x 9" strip from the remaining yardage. Repeat this cutting process for any fabric with a directional print. See Figure 2.

2. Sort the strips into six stacks, each containing identical fabrics. Number the strip stacks 1–6 to match the numbers in your list.

3. Following the chart at right, arrange the strips into eight sets (A–F) and identify each with the appropriate letter on a small piece of masking tape placed in the upper left-hand corner of the first strip in each set. (Set aside the remaining unused strips to use for future projects. You should have one strip each of Fabrics #3 and #6, and two strips each of Fabrics #4 and #5 left over.)

Using ¼" seam allowances, sew the strips together in sets along the long cut edges. Press all the seam allowances in one direction, away from the strip with the masking-tape label. Do not press over the masking tape. Check off each set as you complete it.

Set A   6-1-2-3-4-5-6-1-2; make 2
Set B   1-2-3-4-5-6-1-2-3; make 2
Set C   2-3-4-5-6-1-2-3-4; make 1
Set D   3-4-5-6-1-2-3-4-5; make 1
Set E   4-5-6-1-2-3-4-5-6; make 1
Set F   5-6-1-2-3-4-5-6-1; make 1

4. Stack the sets, right side up, in the order in which they were pieced. The top set should be Set F, and Fabric #5 should be the first (left-hand) strip. Make sure the strip sets are smooth and flat in the stack, with the long edges even and the top edges as even as possible. Place the stacked sets on a cutting board and make a clean cut at the end. Then cut the stacked sets into 2"-wide strips. You will have a total of 32 pieced strips (four groups of eight patchwork strips in each). See Figure 3.

5. Following Figure 4, arrange the strips to create your design. You will need two complete groups of the patchwork strips and some of the strips from each of the remaining two groups.

Note: Use the strips with the identifying masking-tape pieces last so you can refer to them if you get lost.

6. To prepare the strips for sewing together, begin at one side of the arranged strips and stack them in order. Put a safety pin in the top left corner of the first strip in the stack to remind you not to sew a strip to the left edge.

7. To sew, place the first strip with the pin in it, right side up, on the bed of the machine. Place the second strip on top of the first, right sides together. Stitch ¼" from the right-hand edge. As you sew over each pair of seam allowances, gently guide the strips so that the seam intersections match. There is no need to pin. Peek at each intersection as you approach it to make sure the seams match closely.

8. Continue adding strips in the same manner until you have completed the patchwork. Press the seam allowances in one direction, being careful not to distort the completed piece by using too much seam allowance or tugging on it while pressing. See Figure 5.

Note: You have completed what could be the bottom half of a Trip Around the World crib or wall quilt. If you wish to make an entire quilt, repeat the above steps, then join the two pieces of patchwork to complete the quilt top.

9. Remove Squares #1 and #2 from the end of each of two remaining A strip sets. Sew the two strips together, with a #1 square between them. See Figure 6.

10. Sew the resulting strip to the top edge of the patchwork piece, matching the seam intersections carefully. Your patchwork should now have 10 squares down and 15 squares across. Press the seam allowance in one direction. See Figure 7.

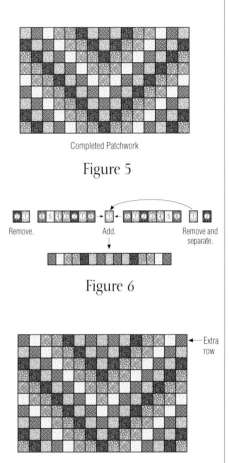

Completed Patchwork

Figure 5

Remove.   Add.   Remove and separate.

Figure 6

← Extra row

Figure 7

Scrappy Log Cabin

This is my favorite patchwork method. It's the foundation for a variety of piecing techniques.

SUPPLIES

1½"-wide strips for log cabin
    center squares
Fabric scraps for logs in a theme
    or color choice plus white
    or a cream color

DIRECTIONS

1. Cut the 1½"-wide strips for the log cabin centers into 1½" squares. Cut a total of 16 squares.

2. Cut a variety of 1"-wide strips from the themed or color fabric scraps for a total of 18 yards. Also cut 18 yards of strips from the white or cream fabrics.

3. Using the chain-piecing method, make 16 log cabin squares. You will add two light strips, followed by two dark strips for each round.

    Place a light-color strip (indicated by a 2) right side up on a flat surface, and place a center square (1) right side down on the strip. Stitch the square to the strip, ¼" from the right-hand edge. Stop; do not lift the presser foot or cut the thread. Place another square

(1) right side down on the strip, touching the square, and stitch. Continue adding squares to the strip, end to end, until the strip runs out. If necessary, add another strip until you have used all 16 squares. Cut the strip between the squares.

4. You will have a series of 2-piece units. To press the seam allowances away from the center square, place the unit so the light strip is on top. Lift the light strip, place the iron tip on the center square, and press out the light strip. Once you develop a rhythm, this task will go quickly.

Note: You may be tempted to iron the units before cutting them apart, but the method just described is easier—and avoids burned fingers.

5. Lay the units right side down and end to end on another light strip (3), with the light pieces (2) going under the needle first. See Figure 1. Stitch; cut the units apart, and press the seam allowances.

Figure 1

Figure 2

6. Lay the units right side down and end to end on a color strip (4), with the light pieces (3) going under the needle first. See Figure 2. Stitch; cut the units apart, and press the seam allowances.

7. Lay the units right side down and end to end on another color strip (5) with the color pieces (4) going under the needle first. See Figure 3. Stitch; cut the units apart, and press the seam allowances.

8. Lay the units right side down and end to end on a light strip (6) with the color pieces (5) going under the needle first. Stitch; cut the units apart, and press the seam allowances.

9. Continue piecing the blocks until you have four rows of light strips on two adjoining sides of the center square and four rows of color strips on the remaining two sides. Make 16 blocks. The blocks should measure 5½" square. If necessary, trim them to a uniform size.

10. Arrange the log cabin blocks into four rows of four blocks each. Sew the rows together.

Figure 4

Figure 3

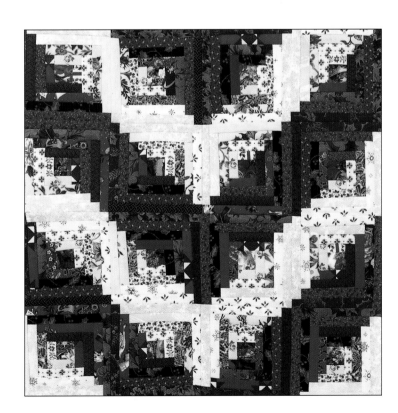

Rail Fence Frenzy

Create a contemporary project when you use bright fabrics to complete these traditional blocks.

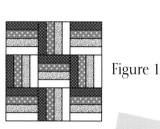

Figure 1

SUPPLIES
See Step 1.

DIRECTIONS

1. Cut 1½"-wide strips, selvage to selvage, from four different fabrics.

2. Sew the four strips together along the long edges, using ¼"-wide seam allowances. Position the fabric strips with the most contrast in either the first or fourth position in the strip-pieced unit. The completed unit should measure 4½" wide.

3. Crosscut the strip-pieced unit into nine 4½" squares.

4. Sew the squares together into three rows, reversing the strip direction in every other block and row. See Figure 1. The nine-block example measures 12" square.

Pieced Fan Pattern

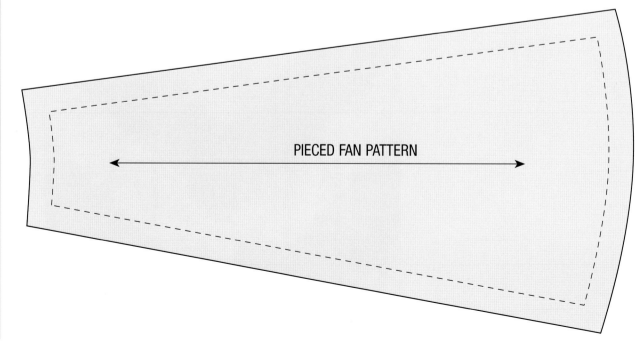

PIECED FAN PATTERN

FABRIC ENHANCEMENT
— PLEATING–TUCKING–FOLDING —

Transform a plain fabric into an interesting part of your project by creating movement with three-dimensional forms.

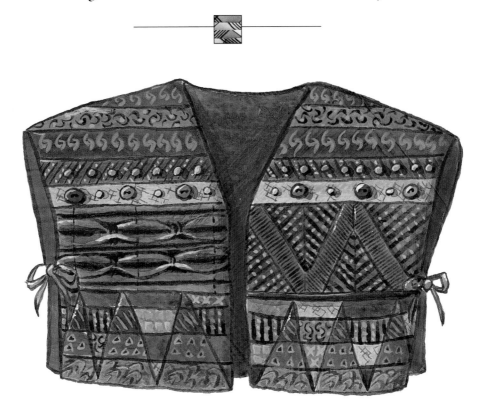

Tabard Techniques:

Couched Tucks–Even

If you need to add some weight or body to a project, try this technique. It's decorative to boot!

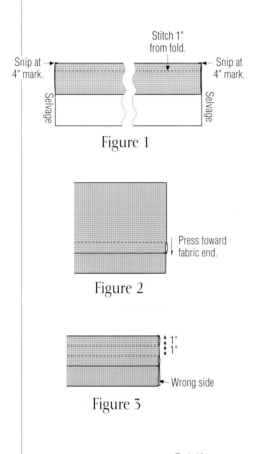

Figure 1

Figure 2
Press toward fabric end.

Figure 3
1"
1"
Wrong side

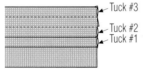

Figure 4
Tuck #3
Tuck #2
Tuck #1

SUPPLIES
⅓ yard of fabric
Approximately 3½ yards of trim or decorative yarn
Thread to match or coordinate with fabric and trim

DIRECTIONS

1. Unfold the fabric and place wrong side up on the ironing board. Measure in 4" from the raw edge at both ends and snip-mark at the selvages. Fold 4" of the top edge of the fabric over onto itself, then press from selvage to selvage along the fold. Pin in place. Thread the machine with matching thread and stitch 1" from the pressed edge. Remove the pins. See Figure 1.

2. With the right side of the fabric against the ironing board, press the stitched tuck toward the nearest edge. See Figure 2.

3. Measure 2" from the stitching and snip-mark the selvages. Fold at the snips, then measure to make sure the fold is 2" from the stitching along the entire length. Press. Stitch 1" from the fold and press the tuck in the same direction as the first. See Figure 3.

4. Repeat Step 3 to make a third, and final, tuck. See Figure 4.

5. To couch trim to the edge of each tuck, thread the machine with matching thread. Set it for a zigzag stitch so the stitches are about ¼" apart (stitch length) and wide enough to catch the edge of the tuck and clear the edge of the decorative cord. The stitch setting will vary, depending on the width of the trim you are using, so it is important to test the stitch settings and practice first on scraps. See Figure 5.

Note: To keep trim from tangling or rolling away, place it in a bag and tape the bag to the edge of your sewing-machine table. Pull the trim from the bag as you stitch.

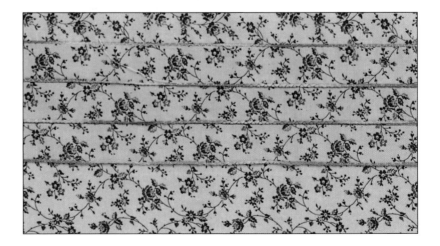

6. Place the first tuck on the bed of the sewing machine under the presser foot, with the remaining fabric to the left of the needle. Arrange the trim snugly against the folded edge of the tuck, with at least 1" of the trim extending behind the presser foot. See Figure 5. (If you have a cording foot for your machine, you can try it for this technique—it frees your hands to guide the fabric.) While holding the trim taut in front of the needle, zigzag the trim in place next to the fold.

7. Couch the remaining tucks in the same manner, being careful to keep the other tucks and the fabric out of the way of the stitching.

8. If you sew the finished patch to another patch, position a piece of cord on top of the visible stitch line, just below the seam line, and couch it in place.

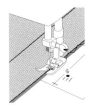

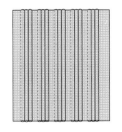

Figure 5

Couched Tucks–Triple

Try this attractive variation on the Couched Tucks— Even technique, opposite.

SUPPLIES
36" x 22" piece of fabric

DIRECTIONS
1. Place the fabric on the ironing board, wrong side up, with the short end parallel with the length of the board. Follow Steps 1–4 for the Couched Tucks—Even version, opposite, making the tucks parallel with the short end of the strip.

2. Next, measure 4½" from the last stitching line and repeat Steps 1–4 for the Couched Tucks—Even version.

3. Repeat Step 2, below left, as many times as needed to create a tucked section that covers the desired area. The finished tucks will be vertical. See Figure 1.

4. Couch trim to the folded edges of each tuck as described in Steps 5–8 for the Couched Tucks—Even version, above.

5. Couch trim onto the first exposed seam of each series of tucks as described in Step 8 for the Couched Tucks—Even version.

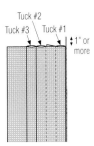

Figure 1

Pleated Perfection

Play with all kinds of fabrics—stripes and plaids, florals and novelties. The effects are always surprising.

SUPPLIES

⅔ yard of fabric—plaids and stripes make interesting effects

⅜ yard of lightweight fusible interfacing

Pleater

DIRECTIONS

Note: You will need the Perfect Pleater or EZE PLEATER designed to make ¼"-deep pleats. A pleater has stiff permanent pleats (or tucks), called "louvers."

1. Cut a piece of fusible interfacing to fit the size of the pleater. The fusible adhesive (rough) side of the interfacing must face up. Set aside for Step 4.

2. Place the pleater on the ironing board with the edges of the louvers facing away from you.

3. You will be pleating the fabric on the bias. Position the fabric wrong side up on top of the pleater, with one corner 1" from the lower right corner of the pleater. See Figure 1.

4. Beginning with the louver closest to you and working from the center out, firmly tuck the fabric into each louver. Use a very thin metal or plastic ruler or a credit card to push the fabric completely into each louver before making the next pleat.

As you make the first tuck, make sure the bottom point of the fabric does not pull up out of position. Use your other hand to hold it in place. Repeat the tucking process until you have made five to eight pleats. Steam-press these pleats in place.

5. Place the lower corner of the fusible interfacing in the corner where you started making the pleats. The fusible adhesive should be facing the fabric.

Note: To continue the pleats, fold the already-pleated fabric and the interfacing away from the pleater and lay the last pleat into the first row of tucks in the pleater.

6. Continue pleating and pressing until you have pleated enough fabric to cover the foundation (use the interfacing as a guide). Apply the interfacing in increments of eight pleats.

Follow the manufacturer's directions for fusing, using adequate steam and pressure for a permanent fuse. Allow the fabric to cool, then turn it over and remove the pleater from the fabric by rolling it away.

Remove the fabric from the pleater and trim it even with the edges of the interfacing.

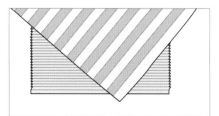

Figure 1

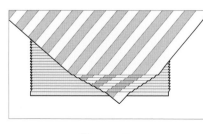

Figure 2

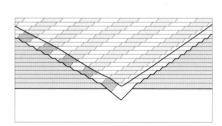

Figure 3

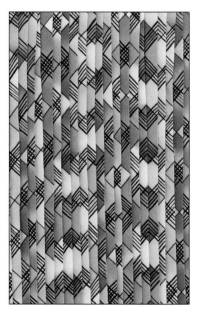

Tucked Medley

You can put together a small quilt in a day's time.
Cover the seams with decorative trims and cordings.

SUPPLIES

Four fabric scraps with length
12" x 12" square of lightweight
   fusible interfacing
Dangling beads
Pleater

DIRECTIONS

Note: You will need the Perfect Pleater or EZE PLEATER designed to make ¼"-deep pleats. A pleater has stiff permanent pleats (or tucks), called "louvers."

1. Place the pleater on your ironing board with the open edges of the louvers facing away from you. Place the strip of fabric right side down on top of the pleater with one short end of the fabric strip parallel to the edge of the pleater.

2. Beginning with the louver closest to you, firmly tuck the fabric into each louver. Use a very thin metal or plastic ruler or a credit card to push the fabric completely into each louver before making the next tuck. When you have tucked the piece of fabric, apply the fusible interfacing to the wrong side of the tucked fabric. Be sure to follow the manufacturer's directions for a permanent fuse. Allow to cool, then roll the fabric from the pleater. Trim excess fabric away around the outer edges of the pleater.

3. Make tucks in each fabric scrap. Cover the butted raw edges of the pleated pieces with ribbon or braid, or a string of beads. Embellish the tucks with single beads if desired. Cover the bottom edge of the pleated section with ribbon, or zigzag over the raw edges of the pleated piece.

Pleated Peek-Thru

This is a great way to use up some larger scraps of outdated fabrics—the pleating changes their appearance.

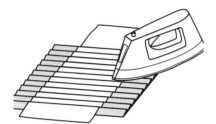

Figure 1

Figure 2

Figure 3

SUPPLIES

¼ yard of Fabric #1
Leftover pleated fabrics or
    12" x 18" fabrics to make
      small new ones
Fusible interfacing
Trim
Pleater

DIRECTIONS

Note: You will need the Perfect Pleater or EZE PLEATER designed to make ¼"-deep pleats. A pleater has stiff permanent pleats (or tucks), called "louvers."

1. To make the peek-thru pleats, use the pleater board and the 12" x 18" pieces of fabric. Each piece will yield a 6" x 12" piece of knife-pleated fabric. Place the pleater board on the ironing board with the louvered edges away from you. Position one of the 12" x 18" pieces of fabric wrong side up, with the 12" edge ready to go in the first louver of the pleater board.

2. Firmly tuck the fabric into the louver closest to you, using a very thin metal plastic ruler or a credit card for best results. Repeat this process, tucking fabric firmly into every louver until you have pleated the entire 18" length of fabric. See Figure 1.

3. Set the iron on cotton (unless you are using a more delicate fabric) and steam-press the pleats while the fabric is still in the louvers. See Figure 2.

4. Cut a strip of fusible interfacing the size of the tucked piece. Place the fusible side against the wrong side of the tucked piece and fuse in place. The interfacing will hold the pleats permanently in place, so be sure to follow the manufacturer's directions for fusing, using adequate steam and pressure. Allow to cool.

5. To remove the pleated fabric, roll the pleater away from it.

6. Decide how many and which shapes you want to use. Trace the desired shapes from page 70 onto template plastic and cut out.

7. Arrange the template shapes on the right side of Fabric #1. See Figure 3. When satisfied with the arrangement, draw around each shape with a sharp pencil.

Cut out each shape, staying ¼" inside the drawn lines. Clip almost to the drawn line at the corners of each shape. See Figure 4.

8. Turn under the raw edges along the drawn lines and press. Arrange a piece of pleated fabric behind the prepared opening and pin in place. Stitch close to the folded edges through all layers. Turn the piece over and trim away the excess pleated fabric close to the stitching. Repeat to complete each of the remaining shapes. See Figure 5.

9. Couch trim around the edges of each shape. To hide the tails of the trim, thread them into a tapestry needle and insert the blunt point of the needle under the edge between the stitches. Bring the point through the fabric and tie the ends off in an overhand knot.

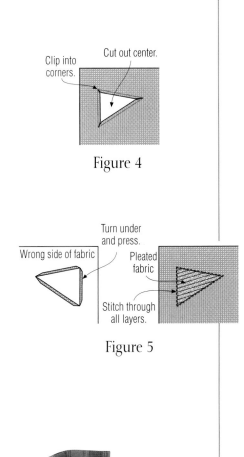

Figure 4

Figure 5

Pleated Ruffles

Pleating the strips at an angle creates fluffy ruffles with an interesting twist.

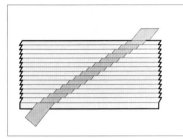

Figure 1

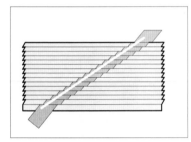

Figure 2

SUPPLIES

3"-wide strip of fabric
¼"-wide strip of lightweight
    fusible interfacing
Pleater

DIRECTIONS

Note: You will need the Perfect Pleater or **EZE PLEATER** designed to make ¼"-deep pleats. A pleater has stiff permanent pleats (or tucks), called "louvers."

1. Fold the 3"-wide strip in half lengthwise, wrong sides together. Press.

2. Place the pleater on the ironing board with the open edges of the louvers facing away from you. Place one end of the folded strip at an angle in the far left corner of the pleater board so that you will be forming pleats diagonally across the pleater. With your fingers, tuck the strip into the first tuck. Repeat this step in every third louver until you reach the end of the board. Press the pleats in place while the fabric is still in the louvers.

3. With the fabric still in the pleater, apply a ¼"-wide strip of fusible interfacing to the strip near the raw edges. Allow the strip to cool and roll it out of the pleater.

Note: If your pleater is not wide enough to accommodate the length of the fabric strip, remove the fused strip and insert the unpleated section into the pleater at the left-hand corner. Continue pleating.

4. Machine-stitch through the interfacing and trim the raw edges of the pleats even with the top edge of the interfacing strip.

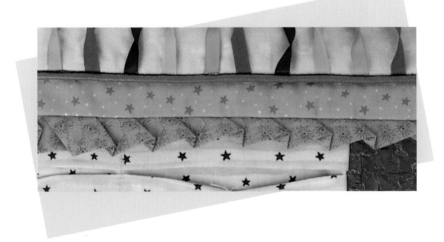

Three-Dimensional Tucks

Use a clean, graphic-print fabric for this technique, and the results will amaze you!

SUPPLIES

Fabric with large-scale uneven print for background
Two fabrics (A and B) for the tucks
Foundation fabric

DIRECTIONS

1. Cut the background fabric in the desired width.

2. Cut the background fabric into 1½"-wide strips, cutting parallel to the selvage edge. As you cut, place the strips face down and keep them in order. This is important! After you make the tucks, you will sew them between the strips in the same order the strips were cut so the original design in the fabric is still obvious even though it is broken by the tucks.

3. Cut ¾"-wide strips from Fabrics A and B for the tucks, cutting from selvage to selvage.

4. With right sides together, sew each strip of A to a strip of B, stitching a scant ¼" from one long edge. Press the seam open or to one side.

5. Now fold the strips in half along the seam line with wrong sides together and press flat. Cut into tucking strips that measure the same length as the strips cut from your background print.

6. Turn the stack of strips cut from the background fabric right side up. The first strip you cut should be on top. Place Strip #1 right side up on your sewing machine. Place a tucking strip on top of it with raw edges even. Place the next background strip face down on the tuck. Stitch ¾6" from the raw edges.

Open out the second background strip and position a tucking strip on top with raw edges even. Make sure that the same color is on top in the tucking strip as in the first one. Place the third background strip face down on the tuck. Stitch a scant ¾6" from the raw edges. Continue in this manner until you have a piece wide enough to work with. Press all tucks in one direction.

7. Stitch the three-dimensional tucks to a foundation, stitching along the top and bottom edges of the tucks.

8. Turn the tucks in the opposite direction from the way they are lying and press. Hand tack them in place from the wrong side of the foundation, or bar tack them from the front by hand or machine, using matching thread and a bead cluster.

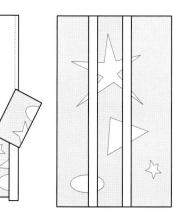

Figure 1

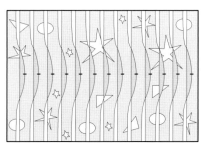

Figure 2

Machine-Grid Smocking

A quick trick that doesn't require the time "real" smocking would. Use it in a sampler quilt or jacket.

Figure 1

Figure 2

SUPPLIES
¾ yard of fabric

DIRECTIONS
1. On the wrong side of an 18" x 25" piece of fabric, draw a grid of vertical and horizontal lines spaced 1" apart.

2. Set your sewing machine for a ¼"-wide zigzag stitch and set the stitch length at 0 or the shortest stitch length available. It may be necessary on some machines to lower the feed dog to achieve this. Or, set your machine for ¼"-wide bar tacking.

3. Thread the machine with regular or decorative thread in a contrasting color.

4. With the wrong side of the fabric facing up, fold along the first vertical line, but do not press a crease. At the first horizontal line intersection, bar tack over the folded edge or make approximately seven zigzag stitches. Without cutting the thread, move down to the next cross mark and stitch in the same manner. Continue down the line until all cross marks are stitched. See Figure 1.

5. Fold along the second line. Tack as described above, but position the stitching halfway between the grid intersections. To make spacing consistent, place the back end of the presser foot at the last drawn line. See Figure 2.

6. Repeat Steps 5 and 6, alternating across the remainder of the fabric.

7. Working from the right side, pull the fabric so the thread tacks show.

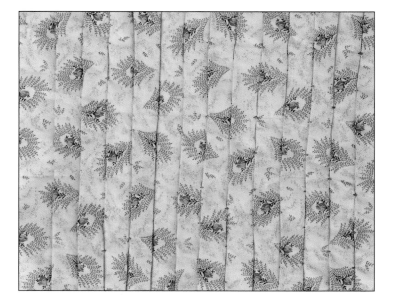

Mock Smock

Press and pleat an evenly striped fabric, and voilá, you have another surface to play with!

SUPPLIES

½ yard of fabric with uniformly spaced vertical stripes (1"- to 2"-wide striped designs are the easiest to handle in this patchwork piece, although for unusual and different effects you can experiment with other vertically oriented designs, including plaids)

DIRECTIONS

1. Leaving a 1" width of fabric flat on both edges, fold, pin, and press uniformly sized box pleats across the width of the fabric. Fold and press along the edge of every other stripe in opposite directions. This will form a box pleat on the right side and tucks of an equal depth on the wrong side.

2. Measure down and mark 3" on every pleat. Stitch across the pleats at the top and bottom edges and every 6" in between, being careful not to twist the edges of the pleats as you stitch across them. Use pins to mark the midpoint between the rows of stitching on each pleat. See Figure 1.

3. Pinch each box pleat together at its midpoint and secure with machine- or hand-bartacking.

To secure pleats by hand, thread a needle with a double strand of sewing thread. Knot. Insert the needle from the wrong side and make three stitches in the same place. Move to the next "pinch" location by carrying the thread horizontally across the right side of the work. Tack as before and continue in the same manner across the piece. Cut the carried threads.

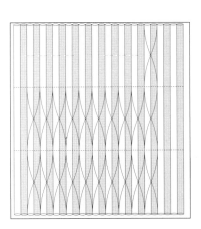

Figure 1

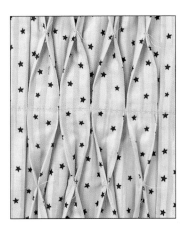

Ribbon Tucking

Be creative with the "ribbons"—try washed bias strips, novelty yarns, and ribbons in different widths.

Figure 1

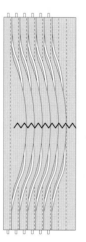

Figure 2

Figure 3

SUPPLIES
18" x 30" piece of fabric
12 yards of ⅛"-wide ribbon, braid, or trim (this may be assorted textures and colors)

DIRECTIONS

1. On the right side of the fabric, make ¼"-long marks at the top and bottom edges of the rectangle. Make the first set of marks 1¾" from the raw edge and space the remaining marks 1¼" apart. See Figure 1.

2. Place the marked rectangle wrong side up on the ironing board, with the short side toward you. Turn the right side of the fabric up to expose the first set of marks (1¼" from the edge). Fold on the marks and press to make a crisp line. Continue pressing folds along the remaining sets of marks. As you work, the newest folded edge will be nearest you and the pressed creases should be lying on top of the remaining uncreased fabric. Be careful not to "unpress" any of the creases you have already made.

3. When pressing is complete, stitch ⅜" from each fold to create a tuck. Press all tucks in one direction.

4. Divide the length of the pleated fabric into four equal parts. Mark by folding and pressing a crease at each division or mark with chalk.

5. Pin a length of ribbon under each tuck at the top edge of the fabric.

6. At each pressed division line, lift the tucks and turn in the opposite direction from the direction the tucks are lying above the division line. As you do this, pull each ribbon from under its tuck and twist it so it lies under the same tuck. At the next division line, reverse direction again so the ribbon is under the tuck. Pin the ribbon in place.

7. Proceed with each remaining tuck and ribbon.

8. Stitch across all tucks and ribbons, using the division lines as the sewing lines. Be sure to stitch across the top and bottom edge as well.

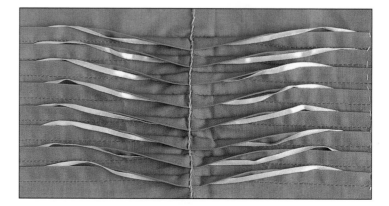

Flat Biscuits

This looks to be an impossible trick, but if you follow the directions exactly you'll get great results.

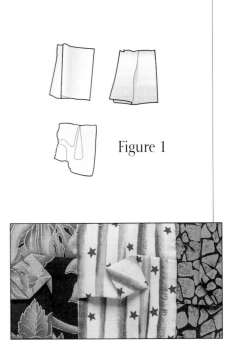

Figure 1

SUPPLIES
⅛ yard muslin or other plain fabric
Twelve 4" squares of two to six different fabrics

DIRECTIONS
1. Cut twelve 3" biscuit backing squares from muslin. Mark the center of each edge of each muslin square. Pin the corners of a 4" biscuit square to the corners of a 3" backing square.

The bisquit square is larger than the backing square, so make a pleat at the center of each edge, with all the pleats pointing in a clockwise direction around the square. Pin in place. See Figure 1.

2. Stitch around the pinned squares ⅛" from the raw edges. Then press each square to flatten out the excess fabric in the top square. Stitch the bicuits together in rows.

Four-Patch Biscuits

Once you have mastered the regular Flat Biscuits, above, start playing with fabric combinations.

SUPPLIES
Large scraps of Fabrics #1 and #2
2½"-wide strip of muslin

DIRECTIONS
1. Cut one 2" x 20" strip each from Fabrics #1 and #2. Using a ¼" seam allowance, stitch the strips, right sides together, along one long edge. Open the strip and press the seam allowances toward the darker fabric. Cut eight 2"-wide segments. Stitch the segments as shown to make a Four-Patch block. Repeat, making a total of four blocks.

2. Cut four 2½" x 2½" squares from muslin for the biscuit foundation. Mark the center of each edge of the muslin square.

3. Pin the corners of the Four-Patch block to the muslin foundation. Make a ½"-deep tuck in one edge of the block; this should be on the seam line. Pin to the muslin at each center mark. Repeat, folding each tuck in the same direction around the square. Stitch ⅛" from the edges. Fold the excess fabric in the center into a square. Press.

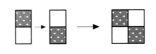

Figure 1

Shark's Teeth

Depending on your fabric choice and pleat depth, this technique can generate lots of surprising results.

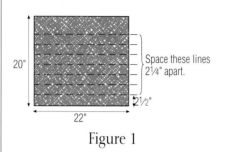

Figure 1

Figure 2

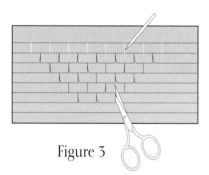

Figure 3

SUPPLIES

⅔ yard of Fabric #1
Scrap of Fabric #2
Scrap of Fabric #3 (solid)
⅛ yard of paper-backed fusible webbing
Tuck and Point Guide

DIRECTIONS

1. From Fabric #1, cut a 20" x 22" piece. Using a chalk pencil or soap sliver, draw a line 2½" above the bottom long edge on the right side of the fabric. Mark six more lines, each 2¼" apart. This will make ¾"-deep tucks. See Figure 1.

2. Place the marked fabric wrong side up on the ironing board. Carefully fold and press along each chalk line, wrong sides together. See Figure 2.

3. Stitch ¾" from each fold line. It's important that this stitching is straight and accurate.

4. Press all tucks toward the bottom edge of the piece.

5. With a chalk pencil or soap sliver, draw a line down the center of the tucks, perpendicular to the stitching.

6. Starting with the bottom tuck, place the Tuck and Point Guide on the tuck, aligning a dot of the guide with the center mark on the tucked fabric. Make sure you are using the correct side of the guide for the ¾" tuck.

7. Make marks at the guide slits of each point desired. (The dots are the center of each point.) Mark only one point on the lowest tuck, two on the next, then additional ones as you move up the piece. Stagger the tuck location as you move up the fabric piece. To stagger, place the guide on top of each tuck, matching the lines with the points of the previous row. Experiment with skipping areas to

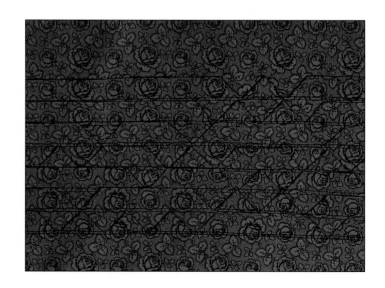

make sections of a row without points. You will be surprised at the interesting patterns you can create with this technique.

8. After marking each point, cut up to, but not through, the stitching on each marked line. See Figure 3.

9. Cut thin strips of paper-backed fusible web. Iron to the underside of the tucks, between the cuts. Do not remove the paper backing yet.

10. At the ironing board, hold the tucked piece so that the underside of each tuck shows. Fold the corner of each slashed edge under toward the stitching, forming a triangle. Remove

the paper backing from the fusible as you press each tuck, not before. Be sure the point of the triangle is true and not squared off at the tip. Press all completed tucks and points flat. See Figure 4.

11. From the right side, triple straight-stitch ½ " away from each original row of tuck stitching, or substitute a narrow zigzag or other decorative stitch if you wish. This stitching catches the raw edge of each triangle under the tuck. See Figure 5.

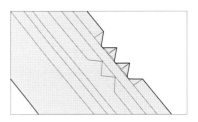

Figure 4

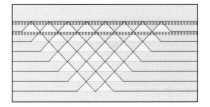

Figure 5

Fabric Embellishing
— Appliqué —

Appliqué adds whimsey to an otherwise plain fabric or block. It can tell a story, you can stuff it, use decorative stitches to apply it, and you can embellish it. It's always fun!

Hat Techniques:

Winding Fan

Create movement on a foundation by piecing small wedges together.

Figure 1

Winding Fan Pattern

SUPPLIES
Small scraps of fabric
Muslin or other foundation fabric
Piping with sew-in seam
    allowance
Template plastic

DIRECTIONS
1. Place the foundation fabric, right side up, on your work surface.

2. Trace the Winding Fan Pattern below left, onto template plastic. Cut 30 to 35 fan pieces from the scraps.

3. Starting at the bottom of the foundation fabric, arrange the fan pieces in a curved pattern. Rotate the wide and narrow ends of the fan pieces to create a gentle curve. Alternate the colors for contrast.

4. When you are pleased with the design, remove the fans from the foundation fabric in order, and stitch them together using a ¼" seam allowance. Press the seam allowances in one direction as you go and periodically lay the patchwork on the background to check the curve. You may find it necessary to add another wedge here and there to maintain the curve.

5. To add piping to the outside edges of the fan, place the piping and fan right sides together and raw edges even. Using a zipper foot or a piping foot, stitch the piping to the fan edges, keeping the stitches close to the piping. Turn the piping out and fold the seam allowances under the fan. Press. See Figure 1.

6. Pin the piped fan to the foundation fabric. Using thread to match the piping and sewing through all layers, stitch in the ditch between the piping and the fan. Press.

Revised Reverse Appliqué

Here's an easy way to appliqué without having to tediously turn under the edges of the patches.

SUPPLIES
Two different fabrics
Fine Fuse (and a Teflon press cloth) or paper-backed fusible web such as Wonder Under

DIRECTIONS
1. Cut your fabrics to the size needed. Following the manufacturer's directions, apply Fine Fuse or paper-backed fusible web to the wrong side of the fabric you want on top. If you use paper-backed fusible web, remove the protective backing after applying it to the fabric. Final fusing will be done in step 5.

2. Layer the two fabrics so the right side of the bottom fabric is against the wrong side of the top fabric. Pin.

3. Using thread in a color that contrasts with the top layer of fabric, machine stitch any pattern you desire. You can either trace pattern shapes on the top fabric or you can follow an existing pattern in the fabric (either the top or bottom fabric). Alternatively, make shapes such as stars, hearts, triangles, or diamonds in a random pattern. Make single or double rows of stitching, as many or as few as you wish.

4. When satisfied with your stitching, cut away the top layer of fabric inside the stitched shapes so the bottom fabric shows through. Be sure to trim close to the stitching. See Figure 1.

5. When the trimming is completed, fuse the two layers by pressing them together.

Figure 1

Fan Appliqué

Make this fun fan, and then embellish it with ribbon, following the technique in this book.

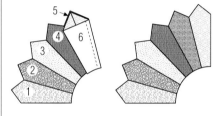

Figure 1

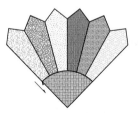

Figure 2

Figure 3

SUPPLIES
Muslin or other foundation fabric
Scraps of seven fabrics for fan
Template plastic

DIRECTIONS

1. Trace Templates A and B from page 82 onto template plastic.

2. Using Template B and scraps, cut six fan blades. Using Template A, cut a fan center from the final scrap fabric.

3. Fold each fan blade right sides together with long edges even. Stitch ¼" from the edge of the wider end of each folded blade. Clip the corners, press the seam allowances open, and turn right side out. Press. See Figure 1.

4. Sew the six blades together along the long edges using a ¼" seam allowance. Press the seam allowances to one side. See Figure 2.

5. With right sides together and raw edges even, pin the fan center to the fan, matching the dot on the fan center to the center seam of the fan. Pin the outer edges of the fan center even with the outer edges of the fan. With the fan on the bottom, stitch ¼" from the raw edges, stretching the fan center as necessary to fit the curved edge of the fan. Press the seam allowances toward the center. Turn under and press ¼" on the fan outer edges. See Figure 3.

6. Position the fan on the foundation fabric. Using a decorative or edge stitch, machine-sew the straight edges of the fan in place. Keep the top of the fan unstitched so you can add ribbon embellishments of your choice.

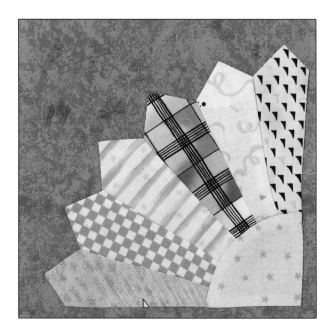

Flowers/Poinsettias

Use these flowers in red and green for a Christmas motif or in bright pastels for a spring or summer motif.

SUPPLIES
¼ yard of Fabric #1 for flower
¼ yard of Fabric #2 for flower
   background
Muslin or other foundation fabric
18 beads

DIRECTIONS

1. Cut two 4½"-wide strips of Fabric #1 from selvage to selvage. Cut twelve 4½" squares from the strips. Make a 1" slit in the center of each square.

2. Cut two 4½"-wide strips of Fabric #2 from selvage to selvage. Cut twelve 4½" squares from the strips.

3. Make plastic or cardboard templates for a circle measuring 3⅞" across and for a 2½" square.

4. With right sides together, pin a Fabric #1 square to a Fabric #2 square for all 12 units. The fabric squares are ⅛" larger than the circle template. Trace around the circle on one side of each unit.

5. Stitch on the traced circle line using a short stitch length. Trim the seam allowance to ⅛".

6. Turn the circle right side out through the slit. Smooth the curve. Press the circle flat.

7. Center the square template on the flower-background (Fabric #2) circle.

Draw a line on the right and left side of eight circles, and on only one side of four circles. These lines are fold lines.

8. Pin two finished circles with the flower-fabric (Fabric #1) sides facing. Stitch the circles together on one side only. Add two more circles. Add a circle with only one fold line to each end. Repeat for a second row. Flaps will stand up in the middle between each two circles. See Figure 1. Press and pin flaps flat on both rows.

9. Pin two rows of flower-fabric circles together. Stitch the rows together just above the flaps. See Figure 2.

10. Pin the flowers right side up on the foundation fabric. Appliqué the outer edges of the circles in place.

11. Stitch three beads to the center of each flower, stitching through the foundation fabric.

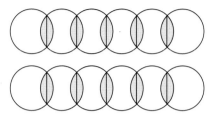

Figure 1

Figure 2

Bow-Tied Packages

Choose seasonal or special-occasion fabrics for the packages and use on Christmas or birthday quilts.

Figure 1

Mark seam intersections
on wrong side.

Figure 2

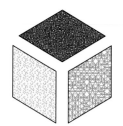

Arrange pieces for 4 "packages."

Figure 3

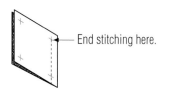

End stitching here.

Figure 4

Stitch.

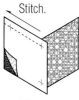

Figure 5

SUPPLIES

1¾" x 14" strip each of a light, medium, and dark fabric
1 yard of ⅛"-wide ribbon or trim to tie bows
⅛ yard of lightweight fusible interfacing
Template plastic

DIRECTIONS

1. Trace the diamond template from page 82 onto template plastic and cut it out.

2. Stack the 1¾"-wide strips on top of each other with right sides facing up and raw edges even. Place the diamond template on top of the strips and cut through all layers, using a rotary cutter and ruler. Repeat three times. You will have four light-, four medium-, and four dark-color diamonds. See Figure 1.

3. Using a ruler and a sharp pencil, mark ¼" seam intersections on the wrong side of each diamond. See Figure 2.

4. Arrange the pieces for a total of four packages. See Figure 3.

5. With right sides together, sew a dark and a medium diamond together for each package, ending the seam at the marked seam intersection. See Figure 4.

6. Add the light diamond, stitching from the seam intersection to the outer edge. See Figure 5.

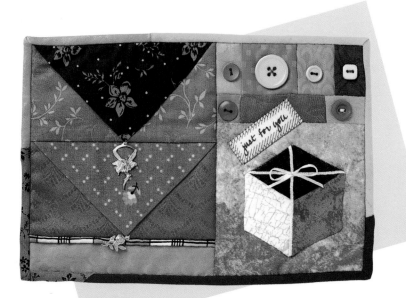

7. Sew the remaining seam, stitching from the center out. Press all the seam allowances toward the dark diamond, which is the package top. See Figure 6. Trim away the seam allowance points that extend beyond the outer edges.

8. Center ribbon or trim over the seam, continuing up to the point. Stitch a second piece across the first, positioning it as shown on the template so the ribbon extends from point to point. See Figure 7.

9. Place each package right side up on the fusible side of the interfacing. Pin in place and cut out. Cut a slit in the interfacing. See Figure 8.

10. With each package right side down on the nonfusible side of its interfacing piece, stitch ¼" from the raw edges around the entire piece. See Figure 8. Trim the corners. Pull the package right side out through the slit. Make sure the points are pushed out smoothly. Press from the right side, making sure that the interfacing does not show at the outer edges. The fusible interfacing will hold the seam allowances and slit opening in place.

11. Hand-appliqué, machine-zigzag, or blanket-stitch around the finished edges of each box. Tack a small matching bow where the ribbons cross. See Figure 9.

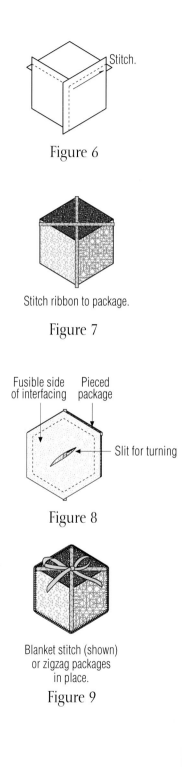

Stitch.

Figure 6

Stitch ribbon to package.

Figure 7

Fusible side of interfacing   Pieced package

Slit for turning

Figure 8

Blanket stitch (shown) or zigzag packages in place.

Figure 9

Patterns

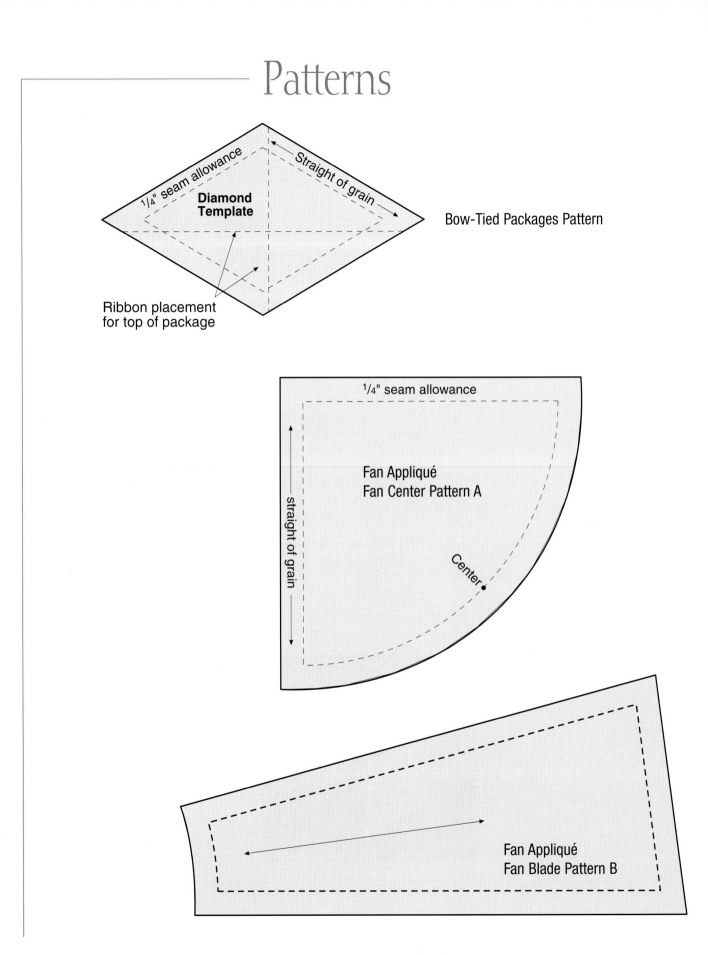

Bow-Tied Packages Pattern

Fan Appliqué
Fan Center Pattern A

Fan Appliqué
Fan Blade Pattern B

FABRIC EMBELLISHING
— STITCHING —

What a colorful way to add excitement to fabric! Search craft stores and needlework and yarn shops to find a wide variety of specialty threads to embellish your fabric.

Jacket Techniques:

Couched Threads

Couch threads onto a plain fabric to serve as a filler and to create texture and interest.

Figure 1

SUPPLIES
⅓ yard each of Fabrics #1 and #2
Decorative thread and couching
    yarn or thread of your choice

DIRECTIONS
1. Cut Fabric #2 for the foundation.

2. Center Fabric #1 piece on top of the foundation piece with right sides facing up. Pin.

3. Replace the regular presser foot on your sewing machine with a couching or zigzag presser foot.

4. Place the ball of couching yarn or thread in a small plastic bag and tape the bag to the table surface in front of your sewing machine. This prevents the ball from rolling around as you stitch.

5. Place the end of the couching yarn on the fabric and zigzag over the yarn to hold it in place. The stitches do not need to penetrate the couching yarn. Stitch 'round and 'round, up and down, anywhere you want to go. Just have fun stitching! See Figure 1.

6. Pin the couched fabric along the edges. Stitch ⅛" from the raw edges.

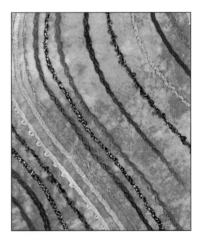

Couched Triangles

This is a fun technique and a great way to use up those little leftover triangles!

SUPPLIES

Solid fabric for background
Muslin or other foundation fabric
12 to 20 small fabric triangles
4" x 7" piece of Fine Fuse
    and a Teflon press cloth*
8 to 10 yards of narrow trim,
    such as Radiance or other
    specialty thread or yarn
*If Fine Fuse is not available in your area, substitute a square of paper-backed fusible web, such as Wonder-Under.

DIRECTIONS

1. Cut the background fabric to the desired size and pin to the foundation. Stitch ¼" from all raw edges to secure the layers.

2. Place the Fine Fuse or paper-backed fusible web on the ironing board with the fusible side up. Place the triangles wrong side down on the fusible and place a Teflon press cloth on top. Fuse for two seconds, or until the fusible is

adhered to the triangles. Allow to cool, then cut out the triangles. See Figure 1.

3. Arrange the triangles on the fabric. If you desire, draw couching lines on the background fabric. Position the triangles so that the edges follow common lines as much as possible. These lines will be covered by couching thread, yarn, or trim. See Figure 2.

4. Fuse the triangles in place. (If you used a paper-backed fusible web, remove the paper first.)

5. Beginning at one raw edge, lay the couching trim in place. Use a tricot or beading foot on your machine if available. It will help guide the trim, leaving both hands free to guide the fabric as you stitch. Zigzag over the trim, being sure to catch the edges of the triangles in the stitching. When completed, all edges of each triangle should be covered by couching.

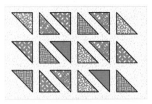

Figure 1

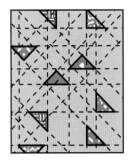

Figure 2

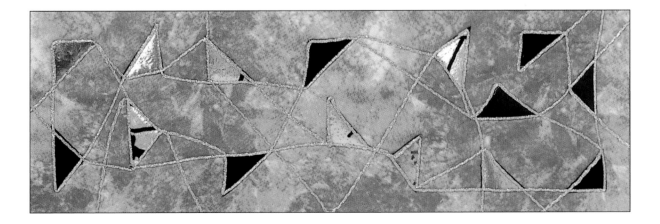

Fused Fragments

If you keep your fabric scraps separate, you will be able to create a picture with the fragments.

Figure 1

SUPPLIES
Fabric scraps
Square of background fabric
Square of Fine Fuse and a Teflon press cloth*
Aleen's Hot Stitch Glue Powder, or small fragments of fusible web
Metallic machine-embroidery thread (or contrasting thread of your choice)
*See note under Supplies, page 85.

DIRECTIONS

1. Following the manufacturer's directions, apply Fine Fuse to the right side of the background-fabric square. Allow to cool. If you are using paper-backed fusible web, remove the paper backing.

2. Cut snips from fabric scraps into confetti-like fragments, using a rotary cutter and mat.

3. Place a thin layer of fragments on the right side of background square. Mix up the fragments, or place fragments of each fabric in individual areas. Shake and mix glue powder with the fragments. See Figure 1.

4. Cover the fragments with the Teflon press cloth (or the release paper from the fusible web), and press with a hot iron. Carefully remove the sheet from the fragments. You may need to scrape some snips off the pressing sheet, replace them onto the background square, and press again with the press cloth.

5. Randomly stitch all over the fragments. Add more stitching to securely anchor the fragments, or for additional embellishment.

Stitched Slivers

Although the instructions call for slivers, you can also add in tiny cut-off snippets for a different effect.

SUPPLIES

Background fabric
Square of Fine Fuse and a Teflon press cloth*
Decorative threads such as metallic or cloisonné threads or metallic ribbon
Fabric slivers
CrossLocked beads
*See note under Supplies, page 85.

DIRECTIONS

1. Place the Teflon press cloth on the ironing board with the piece of Fine Fuse on top. Then place the slivers right side up on the Fine Fuse. Fold the Teflon press cloth so it covers the slivers and any excess Fine Fuse. Following manufacturer's directions, fuse the slivers to the Fine Fuse. See Figure 1. Use a rough sponge to remove any Fine Fuse stuck to the Teflon press cloth.

2. Cut a square from the background fabric. Cut the slivers apart and place them randomly on the right side of the background square. See Figure 2. Fuse them to the square, using the Teflon press cloth to protect the bottom of your iron from any Fine Fuse that might be exposed at the edges of the slivers.

3. Now the fun begins! Randomly stitch over the slivers, adding your choice of decorative elements, including CrossLocked beads, metallic ribbons, and metallic threads. For added interest, you can also use a twin needle and a tucking foot to stitch over the slivers.

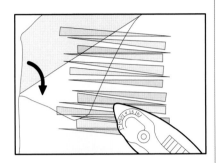

Figure 1

Figure 2

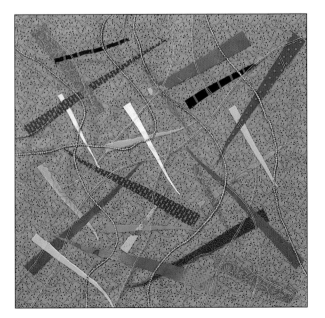

Quilting Crumbs

Don't throw away all those bits and pieces! Fused to a fabric and covered with tulle, they make a great card!

SUPPLIES
Background fabric
Square of Fine Fuse and a Teflon press cloth*
Tulle netting in a dark color
Snips, strips, and threads left over from other patchwork pieces
*See note under Supplies, page 85.

DIRECTIONS
1. Cut rectangles from the background fabric, the tulle, and the Fine Fuse. Apply Fine Fuse to the right side of the background rectangle. If you are using paper-backed fusible web, carefully remove the release paper.

2. To embellish the background rectangle with "crumbs," lay it right side up on a flat surface and randomly scatter fabric snippets and threads over its surface.

3. Place the tulle on top of the "crumbs" and the background fabric.

4. Place the Teflon press cloth on top of the tulle. If you are using paper-backed fusible web, place the release paper on top of the fabric layers. Following the manufacturer's directions, fuse the layers together.

Modified Sashiko

Machine-quilt your bargello, using this simple, elegant, and decorative technique.

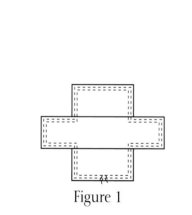

Figure 1

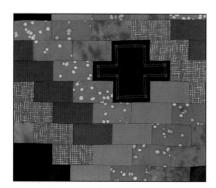

SUPPLIES
Background fabric
Fabric scraps for patches
Twin needles with large eyes (Schmetz 3.0/90 or 100)
Decorative thread in a color that contrasts with fabric

DIRECTIONS
1. Replace your machine's regular needle with a twin needle. Thread the machine with two spools of decorative thread. Use regular thread in the bobbin in a color that matches the fabric.

2. Set the stitch length at 4 to 8 stitches per inch and test on a scrap. You may have to loosen the tension when sewing with a heavy decorative thread.

3. Beginning in the center of one edge, stitch around the patch. See Figure 1. Stitch all the way around, with the outside edge of the presser foot along the edges. For stitches closer to the edge, move the needle position to the right, making sure it will still stitch without hitting the throat plate.

At a corner, raise the needles to pivot. When you insert the needles to continue stitching, insert them in the stitches closest to the edge.

Be sure to leave thread tails at the beginning and end of the stitching. Pull them to the wrong side, tie off close to the foundation, and trim.

FABRIC EMBELLISHING
— WITH RIBBON —

Create magic by folding, twisting, knotting, and gathering all kinds of narrow and wide ribbons. You can outline a seam, cover up a mistake, or simply accent an area with ribbon.

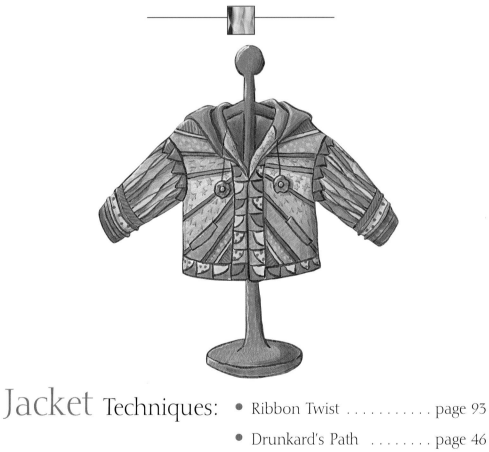

Jacket Techniques:

Box-Pleated Ribbon

Experiment with one of the many ribbons now available to make this favorite decorative trim.

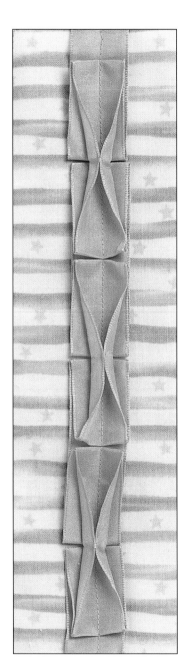

SUPPLIES
Foundation fabric
1"-wide ribbon of any type—wire-edge works well but is not necessary
Cardboard or 1" x 6" C-Thru Ruler

DIRECTIONS
1. Cut a 1" x 4" cardboard box-pleating guide or use a 1" x 6" C-Thru Ruler if you have one. Place the strip or ruler 2" in from one end of the 1"-wide ribbon. Fold the ribbon back on top of the cardboard to the opposite edge of the guide, then back on top of itself. See Figure 1. Carefully remove the cardboard and pin the three layers of ribbon together.

2. Place the cardboard strip under the ribbon next to the first inner fold. Wrap the ribbon under the guide to meet the inner fold, then fold back to complete one box pleat. See Figure 2.

Slide the cardboard out and pin the ribbon layers. You should have a 2"-long box pleat on the top side of the ribbon. See Figure 3.

3. Continue making box pleats until you have enough pleated ribbon to fit the area you wish to embellish. Pin the folded ribbon in place on the foundation fabric. Using matching thread, machine-stitch down the center of the pleats through all layers. See Figure 4.

4. Pinch the top and bottom edges of each pleat together in the center and, using matching thread, whipstitch as shown in Figure 5.

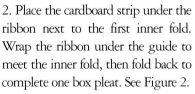

Pleating guide

2"

Fold ribbon back on top of guide.

Figure 1

Fold ribbon back on top of guide.

Figure 2

Box pleat

Figure 3

Machine stitch down center of folded ribbon.

Figure 4

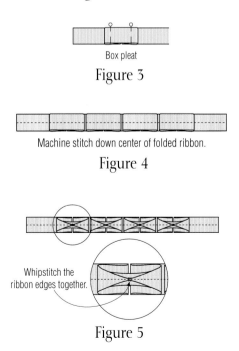

Whipstitch the ribbon edges together.

Figure 5

Antique Ribbon Rose

Make this rose in a variety of ribbons, from narrow for a petite accent to wide for a pretty lapel pin.

SUPPLIES
24" piece of ⅞"-wide
    wired ribbon

DIRECTIONS

1. Fold the ribbon in half crosswise and hold the raw edges with one hand. With the other hand, pull the wires at the bottom edge to gather the ribbon to about one-third its original length. See Figure 1. Unfold the ribbon.

2. Pinch one end of the ribbon and wrap with the wire ¼" from the raw edge. Trim excess wire if necessary. Repeat at the other end. See Figure 2.

3. Fold one end down below the bottom edge of the ribbon and use like a handle. Wrap the ribbon around itself tightly three times. Using matching thread, whipstitch the bottom edges together. Continue to roll the next layer, hand-sewing it just to the previous layer. Gradually move the gathered wire ⅛" out from the previous roll. Keep tacking the rows as you go. See Figure 3.

4. Pull the end of the ribbon to the back and stitch in place.

5. Place the rose in the palm of your hand and squeeze it with your fingertips as if you were squeezing water out of it. Gently shape it and primp the edges, leaving the crinkle in the rose.

6. Pin the rose in place on a foundation with a leaf behind it (see below). Hand stitch the rose and leaf in place from the back side with matching thread and small hidden stitches.

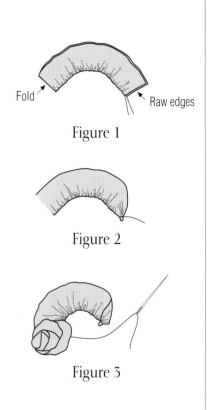

Fold — Raw edges

Figure 1

Figure 2

Figure 3

Ribbon Leaf

Sew one or two leaves behind each Antique Ribbon Rose (see above) for an effective embellishment.

SUPPLIES
2" piece of ⅞"-wide
    wired ribbon

DIRECTIONS

Fold the raw edges on both sides to one finished edge. See Figure 1. Pinch in the center and stitch to hold. See Figure 2. Place under an antique ribbon rose and stitch in place.

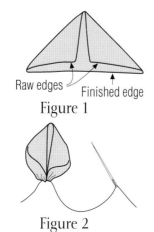

Raw edges — Finished edge

Figure 1

Figure 2

Zigzag Ribbon

A few yards of colorful zigzag ribbon quickly provide a graphic accent to a sleeve cuff or quilt border.

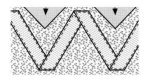

Figure 1

SUPPLIES
Foundation fabric
¼"- to ½"-wide ribbon

DIRECTIONS
1. Position one end of the ribbon at the left edge of the fabric. Bring the ribbon down about 2" to 3". Machine-stitch along one edge of the ribbon. Leave the needle in the fabric and ribbon.

2. Lift the presser foot and pivot the fabric. Fold the ribbon and take it in the opposite direction, zigzag fashion. Stitch the next portion of the ribbon. Leave the needle in the ribbon and fabric. Pivot and repeat the steps until you reach the end of the strip. See Figure 1. Stitch the free edge of the ribbon in place, pivoting as necessary.

Gathered Rosettes

Attach a perky trim of quick-and-easy gathered rosettes to valances or pillows in your favorite girl's room.

Figure 1

Figure 2

—1½" long

Figure 3

SUPPLIES
Foundation fabric
¼"-wide ribbon

DIRECTIONS
1. Pin one end of the ribbon to the foundation fabric. Thread a needle with sewing thread, double, and knot. Stitch through the ribbon to anchor it. After inserting the needle for the second stitch, bring up the needle from the back of the fabric approximately 1" from the stitches. Backstitch again. See Figure 1.

2. Lift the ribbon away from the fabric and sew a 1½"-long row of stitches through the center of the ribbon only. See Figure 2.

3. Draw up the thread tightly to make a tiny gathered rosette. Take two or three stitches close to the first anchor stitch through ribbon and fabric. Insert the needle in the fabric and come out on the back of the fabric. Move forward 1", bring up the needle, and anchor the ribbon with two more backstitches.

4. Repeat Steps 3 and 4 to make the next rosette, continuing until you reach the end of the area you are embellishing. See Figure 3.

Crisscross Hand-Couched Ribbon

This technique works up quickly to cover an area or seam in a straight line.

SUPPLIES
Foundation fabric
¼"- to ½"-wide ribbon
Embroidery floss or perle cotton

DIRECTIONS
Thread a needle with floss or perle cotton thread and anchor one end of the ribbon at the raw edge of the foundation fabric with a few backstitches. Make a large herringbone stitch over the ribbon to hold it in place, catching the finished edges of the ribbon in the backstitches. Referring to Figure 1, bring the needle up at 1, then take a backstitch in the direction of the arrow at 2. Bring the thread over the ribbon to the right; take a backstitch at 3. Continue in the same manner until you reach the end of the ribbon, being careful to evenly space the stitches. Anchor the end of the ribbon with a few backstitches.

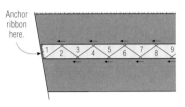

Figure 1

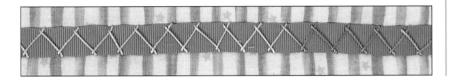

Ribbon Twist

Use this playful trim as a band on a sleeve or as the hem of a special skirt or jacket.

SUPPLIES
Foundation fabric
¼ yard each of four different
    colors of ¼"-wide ribbon
1 yard of piping

DIRECTIONS
1. Cut a strip of fabric in the desired width. Cut lengths of each ribbon, making them each ½" longer than the cut width of the strip. Pin the ribbon lengths to the top edge of the strip, spacing them at 1" to 1½" intervals. Twist each ribbon once and pin the bottom edge to the bottom edge of the strip. Stitch ⅛" from the top and bottom edges of the strip to secure the ribbons. Remove the pins.

2. Add piping to the top and bottom edges of the Ribbon Twist strip. Turn the seam allowances to the back; press. See Figure 1.

3. Pin the Ribbon Twist strip to your foundation fabric. Stitch in-the-ditch along the top and bottom edges, between the piping and the strip.

Figure 1

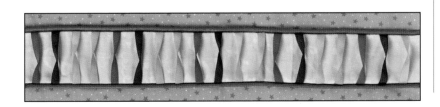

Ruching

Because this is a gathered trim, it will turn corners and go in any direction you need it to.

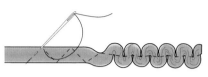

Figure 1

SUPPLIES

½"- to 1"-wide silk or satin ribbon

DIRECTIONS

With matching thread, hand-sew small running stitches in zigzag fashion along the ribbon, leaving the needle and thread attached when you reach the end. See Figure 1. Draw up the thread, gathering the ribbon to fit the fabric or area you wish to embellish. Secure the gathers with a few backstitches. Pin the ruched ribbon to fabric and hand tack in place.

STACKED RUCHING

For a different effect, stack two ribbons of different colors and widths before you do the ruching. Vary the degree of waviness in the ribbon by varying the stitch length and angularity of the zigzag stitching.

Leaf Twist

Embellish your ribbon roses with a few of these easy-to-make leaves.

SUPPLIES

1¼" of ⅛"-wide ribbon

DIRECTIONS

1. Fold the ribbon in half, twisting one end. See Figure 1. Tack the ends together. Tuck a leaf or two behind ribbon roses as you tack them in place, adding a tiny bead or two in the stitching if you wish. The ribbon edge can be stitched in place if you'd rather the leaf loop not be free.

Figure 1

Pinched Couching

This is so easy! Just secure ribbon to a piece of fabric you will use in a project. It's instant enhancement.

SUPPLIES
Background fabric
Ribbon of your choice

DIRECTIONS

1. Thread a needle with a double strand of thread. Place the raw end of the ribbon at the edge of the fabric. Bring the needle through from the back, slightly under one edge of the ribbon. Move the needle across the ribbon and down through the fabric, slightly under the ribbon edge. Take several small stitches over the ribbon, pulling each stitch tight so the ribbon draws in.

2. For the next stitch, bring the needle through the fabric from the wrong side, ½" from the first couching stitches. Stitch across the ribbon as before. See Figure 1. Continue in this manner, couching at ½" intervals until you reach the end of the fabric. If you wish, add beads as you stitch.

Figure 1

Gathered Ribbon Rose

Make lots of these in multiple colors and place them in a row or cluster them together.

SUPPLIES
4" of ¼"-wide ribbon
Background fabric

Figure 1

DIRECTIONS

Fold the ribbon in half crosswise with right sides together. Stitch the short ends together. Make short running stitches along one finished edge of the ribbon, leaving the needle and thread attached. Draw up the stitches to gather the ribbon. See Figure 1. Backstitch to secure.

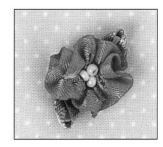

French Knot Bow

This works well in combination with silk-ribbon embroidery work on a dainty blouse or fancy jacket.

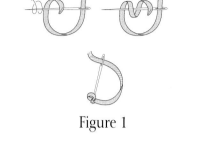

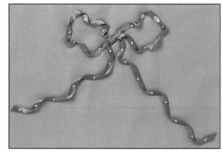

Figure 1

SUPPLIES
26" of ⅛"- to ¼"-wide ribbon
Foundation fabric
Perle cotton

DIRECTIONS

1. Tie the ribbon in a bow with 6" to 7" tails. Using a single strand of matching perle cotton, attach the bow to the desired area of the foundation fabric. Bring up the needle from the wrong side of the fabric into the ribbon. Make a French knot (see Step 2). Twist the ribbon, allowing a little slack, and tack down with another French knot. Continue twisting and tacking at irregular intervals.

2. To make a French knot, thread the needle with perle cotton in a color that matches or contrasts with the ribbon. Bring up the needle through the fabric into the ribbon from the wrong side. Wrap the thread around the needle two or three times. Hold the thread to one side as you insert the needle into the ribbon as close to the starting point as possible. Pull the knot tightly on the needle. Hold the knot in place until the needle is pulled through. See Figure 1.

French Knot Twist

Embellish a patch with a serpentine of ribbon held in place with colorful French knots.

Twist and tack ribbon with French knots.

Figure 1

SUPPLIES
Silk Ribbon
Perle cotton or embroidery floss

DIRECTIONS

Thread a needle with a double strand of perle cotton, embroidery floss, or a single strand of silk ribbon; knot the end. Tuck the end of the ribbon under the edge of the foundation fabric. Bring up the needle from the wrong side of the foundation into the ribbon.

Make a French knot as shown above. Twist the ribbon, allowing a little slack, and tack down with another French knot. Continue twisting the ribbon and tacking it down with a French knot at irregular intervals. If you prefer, substitute small beads for the French knots.

MANIPULATING TECHNIQUES
— BIAS STRIPS —

Cutting fabric on the bias makes the fabric more pliable. It also creates interesting designs in fabric you create from cut and re-sewn stitched strips.

Bib Overall Techniques:

Spiral Bias

Yes, this looks impossible, but the results are stunning. Manipulate the fabric while it's under the machine!

SUPPLIES
⅛ yard each of two different fabrics

DIRECTIONS
1. From each fabric, cut one 4½"-wide strip across the fabric width. Place the strips with right sides together, and stitch ¼" from one long edge. Press the seam allowances toward the darker of the two fabrics.

2. Place the pieced strip on the table, right side up, and make a true bias (45° angle) fold at one end of the strip. Carefully mark point A ¼" from both raw edges at the bottom right corner of the top layer of fabric. See Figure 1.

3. Position the folded strip on the sewing machine and insert the needle in point A. Do not lower the presser foot yet.

4. Without moving the lower layer of fabric, align the bottom edge of the top layer of fabric with the right-side raw edge of the lower layer and lower the presser foot. Pin. See Figure 2. Stitch, even though it appears to be wrong! Continue lining up the raw edges and stitch to the right-side edge of the lower layer. The result is an all-bias tube with the seam at a 45° angle from each folded edge.

5. Press the spiraled tube flat to crease the edges. Cut along both creased edges to create two strips. See Figure 3.

Note: Use this technique to make spiral bias strips for covered piping.

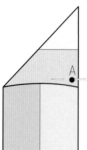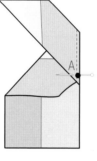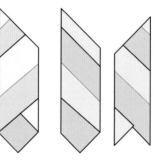

Figure 1   Figure 2   Figure 3

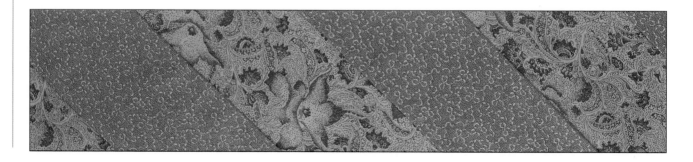

Continuous Bias Patchwork

This technique uses up a lot of leftover strips and scraps you just can't bear to throw away. You'll have a unique fabric.

SUPPLIES
Three strips, each 1½" wide
Four strips, each 2½" wide
Four strips, each 3" wide
Two strips, each 3½" wide
Foundation fabric

DIRECTIONS
1. Arrange the strips with contrasting fabrics next to each other. Sew the strips together, using a ¼" seam allowance. Press the seam allowances in one direction. The piece will measure approximately 27½" x 44". See Figure 1.

2. On one end of the strip set, fold down the top corner so the side edge becomes flush with the bottom edge; press. Cut on the fold. See Figure 2.

3. With right sides together and raw edges even, sew the cutaway triangle to the opposite end of the strip set, aligning like strips. Press the seam allowances open. Position a ruler along the diagonal edge and cut an equal number of 2"-wide bias strips. See Figure 3.

4. Iron a crease down the center of the foundation fabric. Center a 2"-wide pieced strip on the crease; pin. Trim the ends of the strip even with the top and bottom edges of the foundation. See Figure 4.

5. On the foundation, lay a second strip on the first strip, right sides together and raw edges even. Don't match the strips by fabric segments or seams; instead, stagger these features. Pin. Stitch, using a ¼" seam allowance and sewing through all layers. Flip the second strip right side up; press. Trim the strip even with the foundation. Pin in place.

6. Continue adding strips to cover the foundation. Check periodically to make sure the strips are straight. Compensate, if necessary, by taking a deeper seam at one end.

Note: If you stitch a strip to each side of the patchwork, you will make fewer trips to the iron.

7. Trim the patchwork even with the foundation. Stitch ⅛" from the edges.

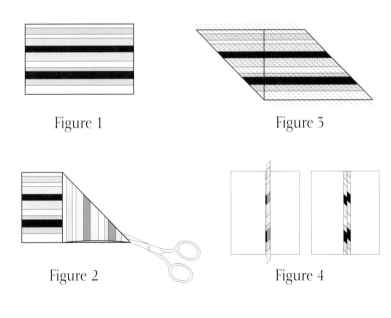

Figure 1

Figure 3

Figure 2

Figure 4

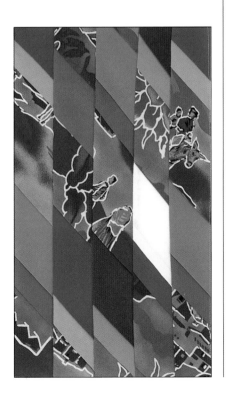

Rose-Petal Trim

This is the sweetest trim to place at the edge of a child's jacket sleeve or to sew around a small gift quilt.

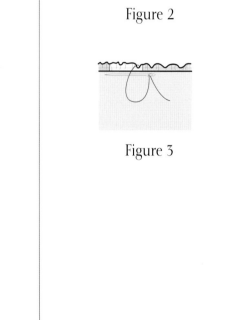

Figure 1

Figure 2

Figure 3

SUPPLIES
¼ yard of fabric

DIRECTIONS

1. Cut 1½"-wide true bias strips from the fabric and join them to make a continuous strip that measures 1½" x 50". See Figure 1. Fold the continuous bias strip in half lengthwise, wrong sides together, but do not press.

2. Attach a gathering foot to your machine. Gather the strip, stitching ¼" from the raw edges. See Figure 2.

3. Pin the gathered strip to the outside edge of the project or garment you wish to embellish, overlapping the strip at the beginning and end. Baste the strip in place using a ¼" seam allowance.

4. With right sides together, pin the lining and the project or garment together at the outside edges. Stitch, using a ¼" seam allowance. Clip any points and curves. Turn the piece right side out. Pull out the ruffle; press.

5. Thread a needle with a double thread, and knot. Insert the needle in the lining at the lower edge of the fabric and bring the thread to the right side at the base of the ruffle, popping the knot to the inside. Stitch over the ruffle two or three times, pulling the thread tight with each stitch. Bring the thread to the lining side and slip the needle between the fabric and the lining, coming to the front ½" from the previous stitching. Stitch over the ruffle two or three times as before. Continue until the edge is complete. See Figure 3.

DIMENSIONAL TECHNIQUES
— PRAIRIE POINTS —

Prairie points were one of the first traditional techniques I learned in my early years of quilt making. Now I use prairie points for a finishing edge and as embellishment in the body of a project.

Jacket Techniques:

Woven Prairie Points

Use these points for quilt or garment finishing—it'll wow everyone!

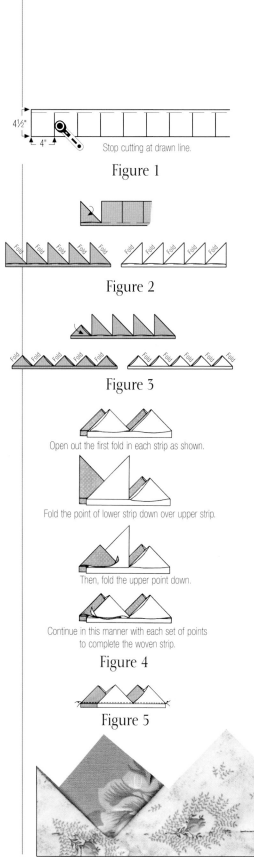

4½"

4"

Stop cutting at drawn line.

Figure 1

Figure 2

Figure 3

Open out the first fold in each strip as shown.

Fold the point of lower strip down over upper strip.

Then, fold the upper point down.

Continue in this manner with each set of points to complete the woven strip.

Figure 4

Figure 5

SUPPLIES
⅛ yard each of two different fabrics

DIRECTIONS

1. Cut a 4½"-wide strip from each of the two fabrics, cutting across the fabric width.

2. On the wrong side of the lightest color strip, mark a line ½" from one long cut edge.

3. Layer the two fabric strips with wrong sides facing up and the marked strip on top. Using a rotary cutter and ruler, make vertical cuts through both layers, spaced every 4", ending each cut at the marked line on the top fabric strip. See Figure 1.

4. Fold back a corner, wrong sides together, on each section of each strip and press. Fold the sections in one strip in the opposite direction to the sections in the other strip. See Figure 2.

5. Fold down the top corner of each section again to complete each point. See Figure 3.

6. To weave the points in each strip together, layer the strips on a flat surface with the folded sides facing up and with the top strip offset slightly to the right. Open out the first fold in each strip. Fold the point of the bottom strip down over the top strip. Then, fold the top point down. Continue in this manner with each set of points to complete the woven strip. See Figure 4.

7. Carefully slide the top layer to the right to center the points along the length of the strip. Pin the layers together, then, using a short stitch length, stitch close along the bottom of the triangles to catch the raw edges. Trim the seam allowance to ¼". See Figure 5.

Continuous Prairie Points

Here's a fast and easy way to make prairie points.

SUPPLIES
⅛ yard of fabric

DIRECTIONS
1. Cut a 3¼"-wide strip across the fabric width. On the wrong side of the fabric, mark a guide line ¼" from one long edge. Using a rotary cutter and a ruler, make vertical cuts every 3", ending each cut at the marked line. See Figure 1.

2. Fold each cut segment in half, wrong sides together. Press. Fold the triangles in half again to complete the prairie points. Press. See Figure 2. Stitch ¼" from the lower edge to hold the folds intact. Trim close to the stitching.

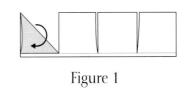

Figure 1

Figure 2

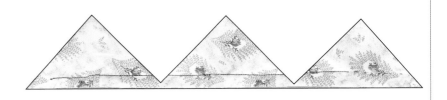

Prairie Points 1

Use this trim as an embellishment in a seam on a garment or quilt.

SUPPLIES
4" x 12" strip of two different fabrics

DIRECTIONS
1. Cut three 4" x 4" squares from each fabric for a total of six squares.

2. Fold the fabric squares diagonally in half from Point 1 to Point 2. See Figure 1. Fold in half again so the resulting folded triangle is 2" wide at the raw edges. Press. See Figure 2.

3. Pin the prairie points even with the seam line, alternating the fabrics. The praire points can be opened to place one corner inside another. See Figure 3.

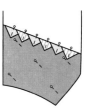

Figure 3

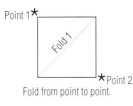

Point 1 ★
Fold 1
★ Point 2
Fold from point to point.

Figure 1

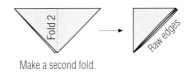

Fold 2
Raw edges
Make a second fold.

Figure 2

Prairie Points 2

Add a little intrigue to your prairie points by placing a vertical opening at center front.

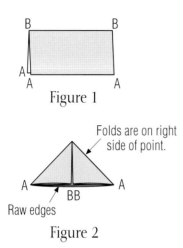

Figure 1

Figure 2

Folds are on right side of point.

Raw edges

SUPPLIES
3" or 4" squares of two fabrics

DIRECTIONS
1. Fold each square in half wrong sides together, making a rectangle with the fold across the top. See Figure 1.

2. Fold each top corner down to the center of the long raw edges. Press. The side with the vertical opening is the right side of the prairie point. See Figure 2.

Triangles from Squares

Here's yet another trick for making prairie points. You can truly use up scraps of any size, color, or print!

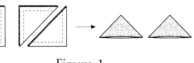

Figure 1

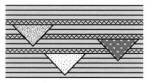

Figure 2

SUPPLIES
Scraps of at least two fabrics

DIRECTIONS
1. For every two triangles, cut two 1⅞" or 2⅜" squares from the two fabrics.

2. Place the squares right sides together and stitch ¼" from all raw edges.

3. Cut the stitched square once diagonally to make two triangles. Clip the corners, turn the triangles right side out; press. See Figure 1.

4. If desired, arrange the points on pleated fabric, tucking the raw edge of each point into a pleat. Using contrasting thread, stitch through each pleat that has a point in it, making sure you catch the point's raw edge in the stitching. Be sure not to stitch over the points of previously placed prairie points. See Figure 2.

Triangles from Triangles

This easy technique shows you how to make perfectly pointed decorative triangles.

SUPPLIES
⅛ yard of desired fabrics
ScrapMaster Cutting Guide

DIRECTIONS
1. Using the ScrapMaster cutting guide, cut 3⅞" triangles from the chosen fabrics. If you prefer, trace and cut a template for cutting the triangles, using the template pattern, right.

2. Fold each triangle in half by bringing together the corners of the longest edge. Stitch ¼" from the shortest side. Clip the corners, turn the point right side out; press. See Figure 1.

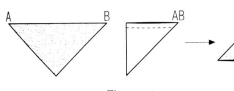

Figure 1

3⅞"

Triangles–Layered

Separate a small triangle that's too close in color to the background fabric by layering a larger one behind it.

SUPPLIES
Scraps of at least two fabrics

DIRECTIONS
1. For every four triangles, cut two 1⅞" and two 2⅜" squares each from two different fabrics.

2. Place different-color squares of the same size with right sides together and stitch ¼" from all raw edges.

3. Cut the stitched squares once diagonally to make four triangles. Clip the corners, turn the triangles right side out; press.

4. Place the small triangle on top of the large triangle with the long raw edges matching. Insert into pleated fabric or seam where desired; stitch. See Figure 1.

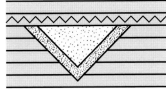

Figure 1

Peekaboo Points

Follow this simple process to make another type of pointed trim for embellishing.

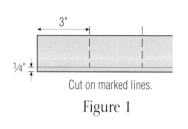
Cut on marked lines.

Figure 1

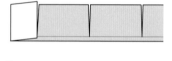

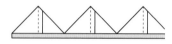

Turn points right side out.

Figure 2

SUPPLIES
2" x 42" strip of fabric that
contrasts with the fabric strip
to which it will be added
Beads, charms, or trinkets
(optional)

DIRECTIONS

1. Cut the 2"-wide strip to match the length of the area you are embellishing. Draw a line ¼" from one long edge. Cut to the line at 3" intervals along the length of the strip. See Figure 1.

2. Fold each rectangle segment in half, right sides together. Stitch ¼" from the top edge. Trim off the corner. Turn each point right side out and press flat. See Figure 2.

3. Place the long raw edge even with the top edge of a fabric strip and stitch ⅛" from the raw edges, then add the fabric strip to the desired location on your project. If desired, add beads, charms, or trinkets to the points. See Figure 3.

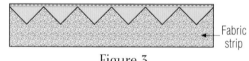
Fabric strip

Figure 3

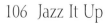

Pointed Tucks

This is one of my favorite techniques. Follow the steps and you can do it, too.

SUPPLIES
2½"-wide fabric strip
Charms or buttons with shanks, about ¼" diameter, to hang from points

DIRECTIONS
1. Cut a 1⅛" x 5" strip from sturdy cardboard.

2. Pin the fabric strip, right side up, to the wide end of the ironing board. Starting 2" from the pins, fold the fabric over the cardboard template to make a 1⅛"-deep tuck. You should have two layers of fabric on top of the cardboard strip and one layer under the cardboard. Press the tuck with the cardboard in place, then remove the cardboard and press the fabric again. Pin the tuck to the layer of fabric underneath.

3. Make another tuck in the same way, ¼" below the folded edge of the first tuck. Continue making and pressing

pleats in the strip until you have tucked the entire strip. See Figure 1.

4. At the sewing machine, remove the pins and fold up the raw side edges of the first pleat so the corners meet in the center. Stitch across the strip, ⅟₁₆" from the raw edges. Press the point flat. Continue folding and stitching the remaining tucks in the same manner. See Figure 2.

5. Beginning with the first tuck, turn the strip back on itself along the stitched edge. Stitch through all layers ³⁄₁₆" from the fold. See Figure 3.

 Repeat with the remaining tucks. After stitching all tucks in this manner, press the strip flat on the triangle side. To hold the pleats in place, stitch ⅛" from the raw edges along each long edge.

6. Once the strip of tucks has been sewn into your project, tack a button or charm to the tip of each point.

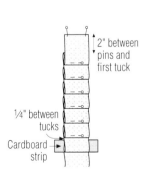

2" between pins and first tuck

¼" between tucks

Cardboard strip

Figure 1

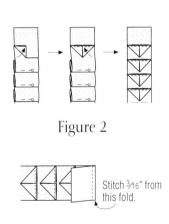

Figure 2

Stitch ³⁄₁₆" from this fold.

Figure 3

My Heart Belongs to Daddy

This row of three-dimensional hearts is a fun insert in a little girl's skirt or jacket.

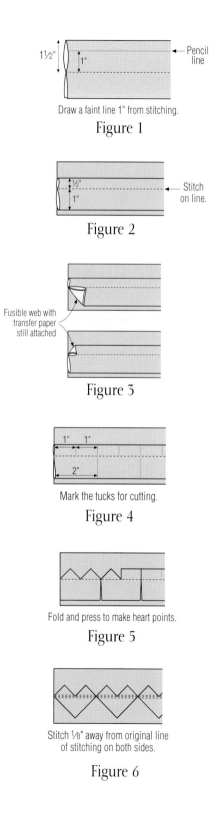

Draw a faint line 1" from stitching.

Figure 1

Stitch on line.

Figure 2

Fusible web with transfer paper still attached

Figure 3

Mark the tucks for cutting.

Figure 4

Fold and press to make heart points.

Figure 5

Stitch 1/8" away from original line of stitching on both sides.

Figure 6

SUPPLIES
5½"-wide strip of fabric for hearts
Two strips of fabric for contrast
Fusible web with paper backing

DIRECTIONS

1. Fold the 5½"-wide strip in half lengthwise, wrong sides together. Stitch 1½" from the fold. Using a sharp pencil, draw a faint line 1" from the stitching. See Figure 1.

2. Open the seam allowances of the strip. Center the drawn line over the seam line, creating an uneven box pleat that measures ½" wide on one side of the seam line and 1" wide on the other side. Press. Using matching thread, stitch on the drawn line. Press. See Figure 2.

3. Cut a ¾"-wide strip of paper-backed fusible web the length of the pleated strip. Apply the fusible web to the underside of the 1"-wide pleat. Cut a ⅜" wide strip of fusible web and apply to the underside of the narrow pleat. Do not remove the backing paper yet. See Figure 3.

4. Mark cutting lines across the wide pleat from fold to fold at 2" intervals. Mark halfway between the 2" marks on the narrow pleat only. Lifting the folded edge with the point of your scissors, cut to the seam line on the marked lines. See Figure 4.

5. Turn down the seam allowance behind the narrow pleat and place the strip on your ironing board. Removing the backing paper one section at a time, turn in the corners of each 1" section to form points. Press, making sure the fusible web adheres. Repeat with all remaining cut edges along the narrow pleat to make the heart points. See Figure 5.

6. Repeat Step 5 for the wide pleat to form the lower point of each heart. Press. Open out the seam allowances of the strip. Stitch ⅛" above and below the center seam line through the backing fabric. See Figure 6.

7. Sew contrasting fabrics to the top and bottom edges of the strip, making sure not to catch the heart points in the seam.

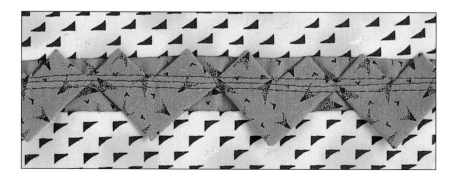

DIMENSIONAL TECHNIQUES

— LAYERING & GATHERING —

Gathering adds texture to fabrics. A sewing machine makes the work quicker and adds the ability to use specialty threads.

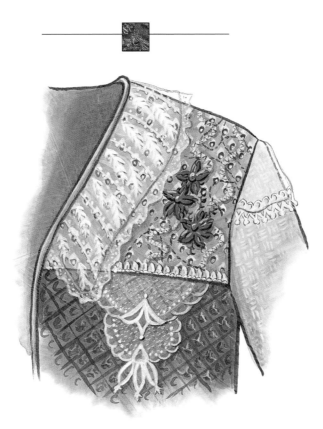

Jacket Techniques:

Stitch and Slash

This method creates a dense padding that could be used for practical as well as decorative hot pads.

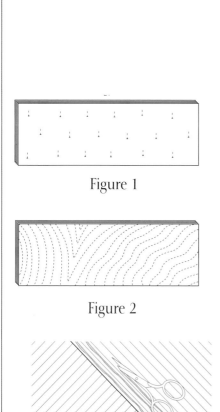

Figure 1

Figure 2

Figure 3

SUPPLIES

7" x 21" piece each of four
  different fabrics
Decorative thread in a
  coordinating color

DIRECTIONS

1. Lay each fabric flat and then layer with the most dominant fabric on top, graduating to the least dominant one on the bottom. Pin the layers together. See Figure 1.

2. Stitch through all four layers, following a design on the top fabric or creating your own design. You may begin stitching from any one of the four raw edges and stitch your design, ending at another raw edge. Space stitching lines approximately ¼" apart to create channels for cutting. Do not stitch across any of the stitching lines. Stitch up and down, and in and out to hold all layers together, always creating channels for cutting. The closer your stitching runs to the bias grain, the less raveling you will get after cutting the channels and washing the piece. See Figure 2.

3. Using small, sharp scissors and beginning at a raw edge, cut through the top three layers of fabric in every stitching channel, being careful not to cut through the bottom layer of fabric. See Figure 3.

4. When the slashing (cutting) is complete, wet the piece only if you used prewashed fabrics. If the fabric has not been prewashed, wash it with detergent. Then place the wet piece in a dryer with a few other items. When completely dry, remove from the dryer and shake to remove loose threads. You may need to trim excess threads.

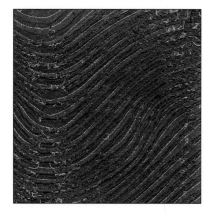

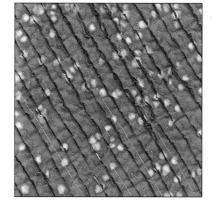

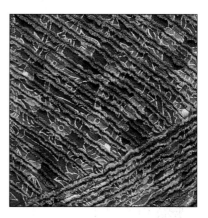

Blooming

Layer several pieces of fabric for a vest; then stitch and cut a design only in the vest's front panels.

SUPPLIES

½ yard each of four to six
  different 100% cotton fabrics

DIRECTIONS

1. Cut a 16" square from each fabric. Decide which fabric you want to use as the bottom layer (lining) of the blooming and set aside. Carefully smoothing each layer in place, make a stack of the remaining squares in the desired order, ending with the fabric you want on top. Be sure the fabric for the top layer has good color penetration on the wrong side.

2. Using a lead or chalk pencil and a ruler, and beginning in the center, draw parallel vertical lines on the top layer of the stack, spacing the lines as close as ½" apart or as far as 1½" apart. Continue drawing parallel vertical lines at consistent intervals. Create a grid by drawing horizontal lines perpendicular to the vertical lines. Draw the first one in the center and work out to the edges. See Figure 1.

Note: For maximum "blooming," draw the lines on the bias rather than the straight grain of the fabric. See Figure 2. On some fabrics, you can follow the printed design.

If you have a quilting-guide attachment for your machine, you only need to draw one horizontal and one vertical line. Then adjust the quilting guide to the desired width to stitch the additional lines.

3. With the lining piece set aside, pin the fabric layers together. Stitch on each marked line, beginning in the center and working out to the edges.

4. Place the stitched fabric stack on a rotary mat. Using a rotary cutter, cut each square diagonally through all layers, cutting all the way into the corners of each square. See Figure 3. Don't worry if you accidentally cut some of the stitches; you will stitch every row again. You may need to use a small scissors to get to some of the corners. See Figure 4.

5. Position and pin the remaining fabric square (lining) on the bottom of the stack with the right side of the lining square against the wrong side of the bottom layer in the slashed piece. Stitch over each row of stitching to attach the bottom layer. You may use a decorative stitch and/or a special thread.

6. Machine wash and dry the stitched-and-cut fabric stack to make it bloom. If you want lots of "fluff" in the finished piece, dry it with jeans and/or clean tennis shoes—the extra friction creates more dimension.

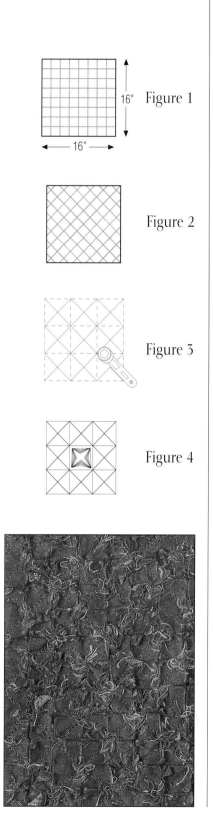

16" 16" Figure 1

Figure 2

Figure 3

Figure 4

Prissy Puffing

Use this application to make dividing strips between blocks, or set a strip between garment sections.

Figure 1

SUPPLIES
¼ yard of fabric

DIRECTIONS
1. Cut 2"-wide strips across the width of the fabric.

2. Attach a gathering foot to your sewing machine and set the machine for the longest stitch length and the tightest tension. Test the stitch on a strip of fabric. The stitching should reduce the length of the strip by one-third. If these settings create gathers that are too tight, reduce first the tension and then the stitch length until the desired results are achieved.

3. Gather both long edges of each strip until they match the desired length.

Note: If you do not have a gathering foot, set your machine for the longest stitch length and the tightest tension. Stitch ⅛" from each raw edge of each strip. On some machines, this causes the fabric to gather on its own. If it doesn't on yours, pull up on the bobbin thread on each side of the strip.

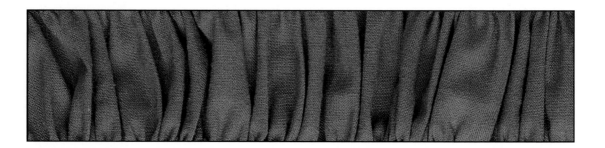

Planned Wrinkles

Once completed, this piece can be cut to any shape or size you need.

SUPPLIES
16" x 20" piece of fusible interfacing
16" x 20" piece of muslin or other foundation fabric
18" x 24" piece of 100% cotton fabric
Decorative thread for stitching
Assorted pieces of cording, narrow braid, ribbon, or silk crochet thread

DIRECTIONS
1. Immerse the 18" x 24" piece of fabric in a sink filled with water. Scrunch and then twist lightly into a ball, squeezing out as much water as possible. See Figure 1. Secure the ball shape with a rubber band or place in the foot of a nylon stocking. Set outside to dry or dry in a dryer with a few towels to help absorb the water and speed up the drying.

2. When the fabric is dry, remove the rubber band and carefully untwist the fabric to preserve the wrinkles. See Figure 2. Place the "scrunched" fabric on top of the 16" x 20" interfacing; place on the foundation and pin along the outside edges. Press to adhere. Allow the wrinkled fabric to dictate the shape it takes.

3. Using metallic, rayon, or other special thread in the sewing machine, stitch the wrinkled fabric to the foundation fabric. Place cording, narrow braid, ribbon, or silk crochet yarns on top of the wrinkled fabric in random patterns, and stitch circles, curves, straight lines, or zigzags to hold them in place.

Note: For a special look on the right side of the fabric, try stitching from the foundation side of the fabric with ribbon floss in the bobbin. Check your sewing machine manual, a book on decorative machine embroidery, or ask your sewing machine dealer how to use specialty threads for decorative effects on the surface of your work.

Figure 1

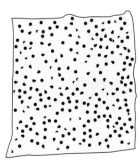

Figure 2

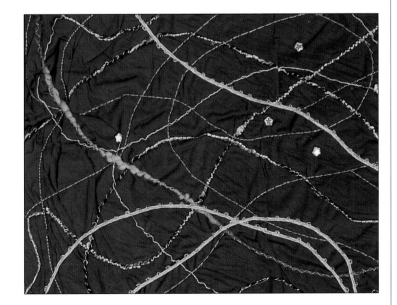

Shirring

Plan ahead when using this technique on a garment. It adds depth to the area where it is applied.

SUPPLIES
Fabric of your choice

DIRECTIONS

1. On the wrong side of the fabric, draw parallel lines spaced 1" apart across the width or length of the fabric. On some fabrics, you can follow the pattern on the fabric instead of drawing the lines. If you use a quilting guide on your machine, it is not necessary to draw these lines.

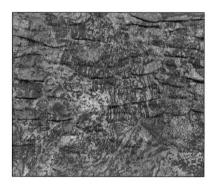

2. Attach a gathering foot to your machine. (Some machines will gather with the regular presser foot when adjustments are made to stitch length and tension.) Set the stitch length as long and the tension as tight as the machine allows. Practice stitching on a scrap of fabric and adjust if necessary so that the piece of gathered fabric is approximately one-third to one-half smaller than it was originally. If your machine is gathering too tightly, shorten the stitch and decrease the tension a notch or two and test again.

3. When you are pleased with the results on your sample, stitch on the drawn lines. After stitching the first line, stitch the remaining lines more slowly, taking time to smooth the fabric in front of the gathering foot to avoid bunching and puckering.

Because the gathering you create with the gathering foot is secured in the stitches, the resulting shirred fabric can be cut and trimmed to any desired size or shape.

DIMENSIONAL TECHNIQUES
— ADD-ONS —

Add-ons bring interest to a patchwork piece. Once I cover a quilt or garment foundation with patchwork, the fun begins as I add other stitching and embellishing techniques.

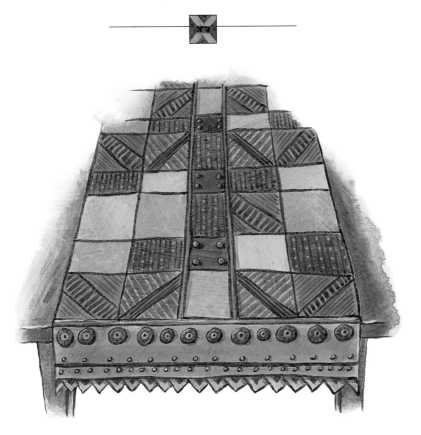

Runner Techniques:

Yo-Yos

Attach a few yo-yos together in a cluster to create a focal point on your project or garment.

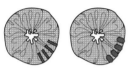

Turn under ⅛"

Figure 1

Figure 2

SUPPLIES
Leftover fabric or patchwork
Circle templates in various sizes
Small beads, buttons, etc.

DIRECTIONS
1. Using 2", 2½", or 3" circle templates of your choice, cut circles from leftover fabric or patchwork.

2. Thread a needle with double thread and knot the ends together. Turn under ⅛" at the edge of a circle to the wrong side, and sew running stitches very close to the folded edge. Draw up the thread tightly, forming a tight circle; backstitch to secure. See Figure 1.

The gathered side is the right side. Make as many yo-yos as you need for your project.

3. Arrange the yo-yos where they will show best. Blindstitch or feather stitch around the outer edge of each yo-yo to hold it in place. Sew several yo yos in a cluster and add beads, charms, or buttons. See Figure 2.

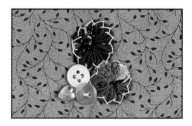

Folded Yo-Yos

These are really quick to make and may be just what you need to spice up a patch that needs a little life.

Figure 1

SUPPLIES
Leftover patchwork
Small beads, buttons, etc.

DIRECTIONS
1. Using 2", 2½", or 3" circle template(s) of your choice, cut several circles from the leftover patchwork pieces, making sure there are at least two fabrics within each circle.

2. Fold the circle in half, then in half again to find the center; finger-press to make a crease. Unfold the circle. Fold the bottom of the circle to the center

as shown in Figure 1. Crease and tack with thread. Continue folding and tacking the right-hand corner to the center until you have six even folds. Attach the yo-yo to the fabric with a button in the center.

Tasseled Triangles

Set the base edge of the triangle into a seam or pleat, either sideways or with the point down.

SUPPLIES

Leftover pieces of strip-pieced fabric
Fabric scrap for triangle facing
Perle cotton or other decorative yarns or threads
Firm cardboard

DIRECTIONS

1. Cut an equilateral triangle from strip-pieced fabric. Cut a facing for the strip-pieced triangle.

2. Place the triangle right sides together with the facing. Stitch two adjoining edges, using a ¼" seam allowance. Clip across the point, turn right side out, and press. Make a buttonhole at the point. See Figure 1.

3. With raw edges even, stitch the open edge of the triangle into a seam. Sew a button in position under the buttonhole and hand sew a tassel in place at the point. See Figure 2.

TO MAKE A TASSEL

1. Cut a piece of firm cardboard the approximate desired length of the finished tassel.

2. Wind yarn or thread of your choice (or a combination) around the cardboard until you have the desired fullness. Slip a piece of yarn under the yarn bundle at one end of the cardbard and tie in a square knot. Cut the yarn bundle at the other end to release the tassel from the cardboard. See Figure 3.

3. Wrap some yarn around the tassel ½" from the tied end to form a neck. Thread yarn into a large-eyed needle and pull up the needle through the neck to the top of the tassel, or add a little white glue to keep the wrapped yarn in place. See Figure 4.

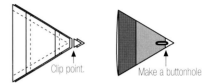

Clip point.   Make a buttonhole.

Figure 1

Figure 2

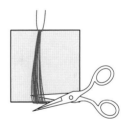

Figure 3

Figure 4

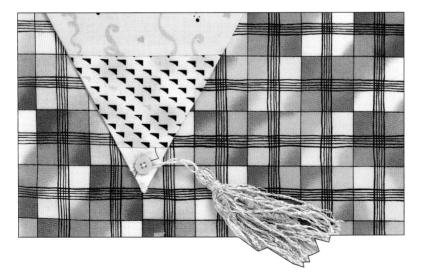

Woven String Strips

This piece will be large enough for a section of a sleeve or quilt, or the front of a garment.

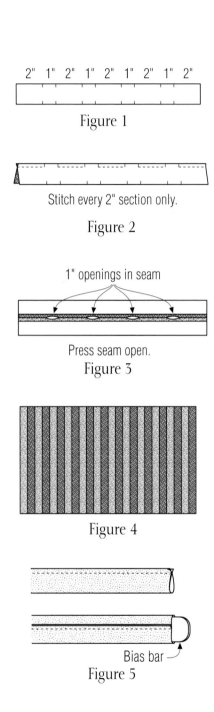

2" 1" 2" 1" 2" 1" 2" 1" 2"

Figure 1

Stitch every 2" section only.

Figure 2

1" openings in seam

Press seam open.
Figure 3

Figure 4

Bias bar
Figure 5

SUPPLIES

Four 1½" x 42" strips of Fabric #1
Four 1½" x 42" strips of Fabric #2
Two 1½" x 42" strips of Fabric #3
Six 1½" x 42" strips of Fabric #4
Beads or button

Note: Fabrics must contrast so that the weaving pattern is visible.

DIRECTIONS

1. Cut each strip of Fabrics #1 and #2 into three 14"-long pieces, for a total of 24 strips.

2. Of Fabrics #1 and #2, choose the fabric on which markings will show the best on the wrong side, then mark each of these 12 strips as shown in Figure 1.

3. Place each Fabric #1 strip face down on a Fabric #2 strip. With the marked strip of each pair face up, stitch ¼" from one set of raw edges in each pair, stitching only the 2"-long sections. See Figure 2. To do this quickly, stop stitching at the mark, lift the presser foot, and pull enough thread to reach to the next mark. Lower the presser foot and continue stitching in the same manner. Clip excess thread between stitched sections. Press the seam allowances open in each pair. See Figure 3.

4. Sew the pairs together to create a finished piece of patchwork. Press all seam allowances open. See Figure 4.

5. Cut each Fabric #3 strip in half to make four strips of equal length, each about 21" long. Fold each strip in half lengthwise and, with wrong sides together, stitch ⅛" from the raw edges, forming four fabric tubes.

6. Insert a ½"-wide bias bar into a strip and bring the seam to the center of the bar. Press the seam allowances to one side. You will have to slide the bias bar along inside the tube as you work since it is shorter than your fabric tube. Repeat with the remaining strips. See Figure 5.

7. Starting at the top edge on the right side of the patchwork fabric, weave a strip in and out through the 1" openings in Row 1 of the patchwork. Begin weaving from the top of the patchwork for Row 2. Repeat the weaving pattern for the next 2 rows. See Figure 6.

8. Fold each Fabric #4 strip in half lengthwise with wrong sides together and stitch ⅛" from the raw edges. Press as described in Step 6.

9. Beginning in the upper left corner and working diagonally from left to right, weave the finished strips of Fabric #4 diagonally under the strips of Fabric #3. Trim excess fabric strip. Skip two patchwork strips before starting to weave the second strip. Continue weaving with the strips until you have woven eight or nine strips. See Figure 7.

10. Now weave with the strips of Fabric #4 in the opposite diagonal direction, running the strips over the first strips of Fabric #2. The strips should create an X on top of the patchwork fabric and go under a Fabric #3 strip where they cross. See Figure 8.

11. Add a bead, button, or embellishment of your choice at each intersection where Fabric #4 strips meet under Fabric #3 strips.

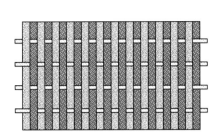

Figure 6

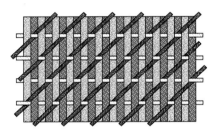

Figure 7

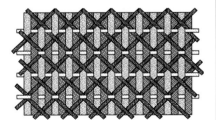

Figure 8

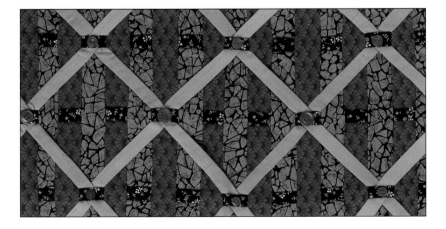

Knotted Tubes

Make 4½" knotted-tube blocks and use 4½" blocks in plain fabrics of contrasting colors to form a patchwork.

Figure 1

SUPPLIES
1½"-wide strip each of
   Fabrics A and B
4½"-wide strip of contrasting
   fabric

DIRECTIONS

1. Pin the 1½"-wide strips with right sides together and stitch along the long raw edges. Turn the tube right side out and press. See Figure 1.

Note: To make it easy to turn the tube right side out, stitch with a cord inside. Use several stitches to secure the cord at one end of the tube. Pull the other end of the cord to turn the tube right side out.

2. Cut the finished tube into 6" lengths.

3. Tie a knot in each tube, spacing the knots at different levels on each tube. Tie some tubes so fabric A is the knot and fabric B is the strip showing above and below the knot. Tie others so fabric B is the knot and fabric A shows above and below the knot. Or, tie and position so that fabric A shows above the knot and B shows below the knot, or vice versa.

4. Pin the knotted tubes across a 4½"-wide fabric strip, and stitch across the tube ends to hold them in place. Trim the ends even with the strip edges.

Woven Patch Closure

This unique as well as functional garment closure can also enhance a purse or pocket flaps.

SUPPLIES

¼ yard each of four high-contrast fabrics
Two or three ½"-diameter buttons

DIRECTIONS

1. Select two different fabrics for the tabbed closures. From each fabric, cut a 4½"- to 5-wide piece long enough to cross over the background fabric.

2. Fold each of the two fabrics in half lengthwise, right sides together, and cut a point at one end as shown. Stitch ¼" from the long raw edge, leaving the short end open. Clip the corners, turn right side out, and press. See Figure 1.

3. Position the finished tabs across the desired location, leaving at least 1" of space between them. Pin in place, then stitch ¼" from the raw edges. See Figure 2 for an example of how to use the closure.

4. For the weaving strips, cut 2 strips of fabric long enough to reach from above the top edge of the top closure strip to beyond the bottom edge of the bottom closure strip. Fold each strip in half lengthwise with right sides together, and stitch ¼" from the long raw edges. Turn right side out and press. See Figure 3.

5. Weave the finished strips in and out of the tabs, leaving some of the background fabric showing in between strips. Pin in place. Stitch the top and bottom ends of the weaving strips in place ⅛" from the raw edges.

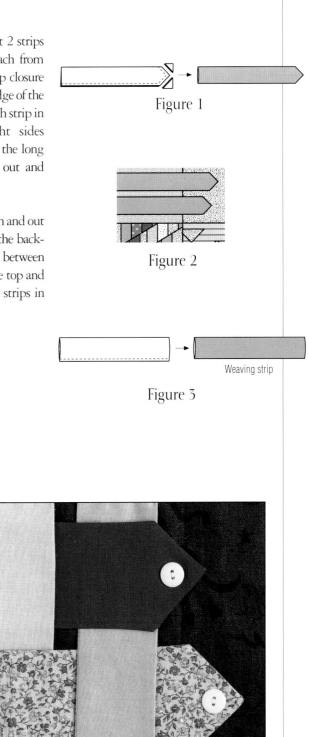

Figure 1

Figure 2

Figure 3

Weaving strip

JUDY'S TIPS & TRICKS

Before you begin a project, make a **swatch card** to identify each of your fabrics. Cut a small swatch of each fabric and label it appropriately (A, B, C for the prints and #1, #2, #3 for the solids). Staple the swatches to your card, along with any coordinating trims. When you need to shop for additional fabrics, your card will be a handy reference tool.

If you plan to use tissue lamé, metallics, or other fabrics that ravel, apply a lightweight **fusible interfacing** to the wrong side before cutting any of the pieces. To avoid melting or puckering delicate fabrics, choose a cool-fuse interfacing—ask for it at your favorite fabric store. Be sure to follow the manufacturer's directions when fusing.

When working Striking Stripes, page 20, or another technique that calls for **striped fabrics**, into your project, select the striped fabrics first and then pick out your other fabrics to match. It is usually more difficult the find striped fabrics after you've chosen all other fabrics.

To make a patchwork area interesting, try
silk-flower appliqué using silk
flowers from crafts shops. The flower parts, with a
few leaves, are all you need. Sometimes the crafts
shops sell flowers that have pulled away from the stems
as damaged and you can pick them up inexpensively.

Take the silk flowers apart by pulling out the
plastic centers. Discard the centers. From each bloom, you should have three to five
flower pieces. Press the pieces. Pin the flowers to the background fabric. Occasionaly place a
smaller flower on top of a contrasting larger one. Play with the arrangement until you're
pleased with the design. Use enough fine pins to hold the flowers securely in place.

Machine-stitch the flowers to the background, using machine-embroidery thread and
buttonhole stitches. If your machine doesn't have a buttonhole stitch, use a ⅛"-wide zigzag
stitch. When you have finished stitching, pull the thread ends to the back and tie off. Remove
the work from the machine.

Place a flower section in an embroidery hoop, and add French knots to the center of each
flower. Bring the ribbon or thread to the wrong side and backstitch to anchor before cutting.

Buy a widely varied selection of
ribbons and trims in
1- to 3-yard cuts so that you have
plenty to work with as you
embellish your patchwork.

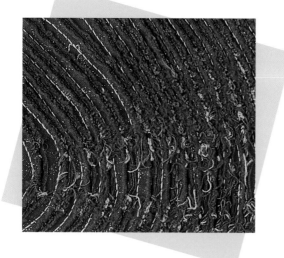

When working Stitch and Slash, page 110, or Blooming, page 111, into your project, select fabrics that have good color penetration on both the right as well as the wrong side for a rich look. Avoid fabrics with a wrong side that is white or substantially lighter than the right side because it will show when the blooming or slashing is completed.

Decorative top-stitching will greatly enhance the pieced surface of your project. If you would like to experiment with Ribbon Floss, hand wind it onto a bobbin. If your machine has a bobbin case, purchase an extra bobbin case and loosen the tension screw so the Ribbon Floss slides through easily. Stitch with the foundation side up. You will be stitching "blind," so do a test first to see if you like the results. Also, experiment with different stitches.

You can also add decorative stitching to the surface of your project by stitching over threads or ribbons from the top. Arrange the decorative thread, ribbon, or cord in the area you wish to embellish and stitch over it with another thread, using a regular zigzag setting. For this technique, you can use textured yarns and decorative threads that might not work in the bobbin. If your sewing machine has built-in embroidery stitches, try them too. Use a decorative thread, such as a rayon machine-embroidery or metallic thread, on top and regular thread in the bobbin. A contrast in texture and color adds more interest to the finished work. If you want only the decorative yarn to show, use a matching thread.

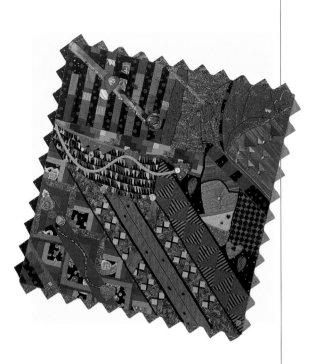

To apply, use an all-pupose sewing or cording foot. Adjust your sewing machine's zigzag-width setting to clear just the width of the decorative yarn or thread you will stitch over. To begin, pull about 3" of yarn behind the foot and begin to zigzag over the yarn, holding it taut in front of the foot. The needle and presser foot will do the work as you keep the yarn centered under the foot. If your machine has a couching/braiding foot, use it. It holds the yarn in front of the foot, freeing your hands for maneuvering the fabric. Leave a tail of yarn at the end of the couching to thread through a large needle, bring to the other side, and tie off.

If you must clean your finished project, be sure to ask the dry cleaner to clean and steam only. Pressing can ruin the beautiful patchwork and textures you've so carefully created on the surface of your project. If you are careful to spot-clean your project whenever necessary, you can keep dry cleaning to a minimum.

INDEX

MARTINGALE & COMPANY
SELECT PUBLICATIONS

HOLIDAY QUILTS AND CRAFTS
Appliquilt® for Christmas • Tonee White
Coxcomb Quilt • Donna Hanson Eines
Easy Seasonal Wall Quilts
   • Deborah J. Moffett Hall
Folded Fabric Fun • Nancy J. Martin
Quick-Sew Celebrations
Quilted for Christmas
Quilted for Christmas, Book II
Quilted for Christmas, Book III
Quilted for Christmas, Book IV
Welcome to the North Pole
   • Piece O' Cake Designs, Inc.

HOME DECORATING
Decorate with Quilts & Collections
   • Nancy J. Martin
The Home Decorator's Stamping Book
   • Linda Barker
Living with Little Quilts • Alice Berg,
   Mary Ellen Von Holt &
   Sylvia Johnson
Make Room for Quilts • Nancy J. Martin
Soft Furnishings for Your Home
   • Sharyn Skrabanich
Welcome Home™: Debbie Mumm

STITCHERY/NEEDLE ARTS
Baltimore Bouquets • Mimi Dietrich
Crazy but Piecable • Hollie A. Milne
Christmas Ribbonry • Camela Nitschke
*Hand-Stitched Samplers from I Done
   My Best* • Saundra White
Machine Needlelace • Judy Simmons
Miniature Baltimore Album Quilts
   • Jenifer Buechel
A Passion for Ribbonry
   • Camela Nitschke
A Silk-Ribbon Album • Jenifer Buechel
Victorian Elegance • Lezette Thomason

WEARABLES
Crazy Rags • Deborah Brunner
Dress Daze • Judy Murrah
Dressed by the Best
Easy Reversible Vests • Carol Doak
Jacket Jazz • Judy Murrah
Jacket Jazz Encore • Judy Murrah
More Jazz from Judy Murrah
Quick-Sew Fleece
Sew a Work of Art Inside and Out
   • Charlotte Bird
Variations in Chenille • Nanette Holmberg

Many of these books are available at your local
fabric, quilt, or craft shop. For more information,
call, write, fax, or e-mail for a free color catalog.

Martingale & Company
PO Box 118
Bothell, WA 98041-0118 USA

Toll-free: 1-800-426-3126
Int'l: 425-483-3313
24-Hour Fax: 425-486-7596
E-mail: info@patchwork.com
Web: www.patchwork.com